My Monk

my monk

A TYPOGRAPHIC NOVEL

Elizabeth Dembrowsky

Copyright © 2009 Elizabeth Dembrowsky

All rights reserved. No part of this book may be reproduced or transmitted in any form or by any means, electronic or mechanical, including photocopying, recording or by an information storage or retrieval system now known or heretoafter invented – except by a reviewer who may quote brief passages in a review to be printed in a magazine or newspaper – without permission in writing from the publisher.

For information address Heliotrope Books 125 East 4th Street, New York, NY 10003.

Cover illustration by Claire E. Keys
Back cover photograph courtesy of Adriana Gheorghe
Author photograph on page 301 courtesy of Judy Rosenblatt
Interior typesetting by Elizabeth Dembrowsky and Naomi Rosenblatt

Spot illustrations on pages 163 and 172 by Claire E. Keys
Spot illustration on page 196 by Naomi Rosenblatt

For Brenda:

Thanks for all the ~~fish~~
back-porch laughter and tears

When a Jew prays, he is asking God *(sic)* a question that has no end.
—Nicole Krauss, *The History of Love*

1

I believe(d) in love at first sight. It happened to me. He became a monk. ~~I came back to America.~~

~~I went back to America.~~

~~I returned to America.~~

I came back to America.

>(Way to begin a novel! Broken heart...)

I don't believe in G-d, but on the days that I do,

>(Yes, that is a contradiction – astute of you to notice.

>>(Sorry. I can be a real jerk. I like to blame my older brother and the fact that I was a competitive child; I learned to make quick quips at an early age, and, as I have moved slowly – kicking and screaming – into the arena of adulthood, I often am unable to

stifle my sarcastic side. Some people enjoy it and give it right back at me, and others find it "very annoying" or even "outright rude."

I acknowledge sarcasm for what it is: A self-defense mechanism that has become a habit. If you keep people at an arm's length – or further – it is difficult for them to punch you in the gut

(unless, of course, they have really long arms

(in which case, run!))

I'm trying to work on it, but, as with most things I try, it is a work in progress. At least I have warned you.).

(However, in my defense, Oscar Wilde said, "Consistency is the last refuge of the unimaginative." Arthur Burgess claimed that a writer who never contradicted himself

(Harriet[1] finds room in her Third Wave Feminist[2] heart to forgive his insistence on such limiting gender specific terms)

is never re-read.)

---

[1] Harriet is the main character in this novel. Although the novel is called *My Monk in Garamond*, the book is about Harriet. "I" am the narrator. I am not Harriet. I do not really even exist. I am, for lack of a better word, a "device" to assist with this particular form of storytelling. This book could have been written in first person, giving you the impression that Harriet was telling you her own story, as at the beginning of the novel, the part that you have read thus

far and for the next several pages – but only because it worked as a means to lure you, the reader, into the action. Or so I hope. Well, you are still here, so it must have done something. But maybe you are only here because you have to read this for school. Yeah, right! Way wishful thinking, but maybe if you are in the United Kingdom, you will have to read this for school – as it appears a large percentage of the Comparative Literature currently being studied at universities across the U.K. include a lot of American writers of the past seventy-five or so years, so at least I have a crying chance at being that sort of specimen.

I could have written in second person – a tricky thing – telling the story as if you, the reader, were experiencing it. Don't get it? Well, think of those *Choose Your Own Adventure* stories.

It would have been written in third person limited – telling you what is happening to the characters but not getting into the hearts, minds, and souls of the characters, but that method is oh-so-boring.

It should have been written in third person omniscient – giving you insight into all the characters – but, as there is only one consistent character the decision was made to give the narrator a personality; even if it can be an annoying one at times – that was the decision.

It's sort of a *Harriet the Spy* meets Dostoyevsky's narrators at the laundromat located on the corner of 30th Ave and 49th in Queens, and they meet up with John Ray Jr., Ph.D. and discuss existentialism over Marlboro Lights while waiting for the rinse cycle to complete.

On occasion, the narrator tells us what Harriet thinks, but how does the narrator really know? Is the narrator simply projecting his/her/their/its ideas/opinions/experiences/fetishes/interpretations/insecurities/passions onto sweet, little Harriet?

In any case, Harriet is the protagonist; well, she is meant to be the protagonist. You may end up concluding that she is also the antagonist, but I will leave that up for you to decide. But who am I? And who are you for that matter? And how are you by the way, sorry for taking so long to ask. And where are you? When are you? And most importantly WHY WHY WHY?

[2]Harriet practices her own form of Third Wave Feminism. In any case, Harriet's Third Wave Feminism acknowledges that many of the women she so admired in high school and early college have led her astray. These women include Ani DiFranco, Gloria Steinem, Marge Piercy, Dorothy Parker, and she even places

On the days that I do believe in G-d, I think He has a fantastic sense of humor. I imagine Him up in heaven, getting bored with things and then sweeping aside the clouds to look down on the little ball, known in English, as Earth.

Inevitably, He focuses on one Harriet Zabrosky – clumsy, great-hearted mass of misplaced energy that she is. He laughs to himself – thinking of all the trials He has sent her – His little, female, 21st century Job –

- The broken cars,
- The misplaced keys,
- The stolen wallets.

Ha ha, He laughs, remembering the 'incident' in that jazz bar in Roxbury. The one where she worked during college.

(Wally's Cafe, right on Mass Ave. between the Orange Line stop and Tremont Street.)

Yes, He remembers.

(G-d has a great memory

(I tend to believe, on those days that I do believe).)

---

blame on poor, long-dead Jane Austen. She has learned, the hard way, that although "The Man" (the metaphorical one) may indeed be "trying to keep her down," reminding him (a real, physical one) relentlessly does not bode well for a decent, harmonious relationship.

He remembers that chess player he sent in. He remembers Harriet in her "fiercely bleeding-heart stage." She offered to play chess on her birthday with that man. She knew he was "sketchy," but she refused to admit it. She played the "Intentionally Naive Card" that she seems to favor and sat down.

Not only did the man leave the bar as the champion of the game, but he took her little purse with him – full of free makeup from *Lancome* and her newly-cashed paycheck. The bouncer, a very gentle and sweet black man of something in the range of 300 pounds and standing at six foot three, scolded her for bringing that much cash into the bar. She didn't bother with her "Is it a crime to be trusting?" lecture.

(By the way, it is a crime to be trusting, at least according to the tone of voice of the hostel manager in London where Harriet's laptop was stolen

(and her passport as well).

(Yes, this is all true.))

G-d looks down and remembers the fun in having timed the day that Harriet endeavored to purchase her first bed – a beautiful, full-size, red, cherry frame, a sled-design – from that nice, independently owned furniture store on Geary Street in San Francisco, to also be the day that her boss, the Director of the Research Department of the Health Care Institute, was to tell her that rather than give her the health insurance she had been without for almost two years now, that she was going to hire a different temp to fill the position.

G-d remembers the boss telling Harriet she felt that Harriet was "going to do great things," not specifically stating that these great things were not to be done there in the Research Department office as a Senior Administrative Assistant.

The boss probably liked Harriet because she was energetic, assertive, and optimistic. The boss, a German anglophile, with bangs and a broad forehead, used to make excuses to come in and speak with Harriet, finding her a willing listener and a nice girl.

Harriet didn't know how to act as a Senior Administrative Assistant. Should she should feign interest in her boss talking about a recent trip to Costa Rica with some travel group?

(Harriet can be a bit aloof.)

Harriet had lived in Central America, twice, in the country of Belize both times. She had suffered through a bot-fly growing in her scalp, "falling in love," for the second[3] time in her life, with a Rastafarian boy

(who described her blue eyes as grey

(and ended up going to jail for drug dealing

(but still was sweet enough to write her a letter from the prison in Hattieville

(the one alongside the Western Highway)

---

[3] Harriet's first love was her dog. She married him when she was young. A man who Harriet met in Williamsburg, Brooklyn told her that when he was young he married his cat.

to tell her he was sorry for what happened in New York

> (He was referring to the September 11th attacks on the World Trade Center.)))),

and flying in an eight-seat plane with a seatbelt held together by duct tape, leaning out of an open door, shooting video footage of the Belize River and of the soon-to-be-official national park located in San Antonio, down in the southern part of the Cayo District.

(Yes, this is all true.)

She had lived in a tent for three months, without running water, frequently hiking down to the Sibun River to bathe. She had carried a graduate student a three-quarter-mile trek through the jungles after the woman had twisted her ankle. She had seen, up-close, a bug the size of a dinner plate while sitting very still in a deep, dark cave. She had witnessed a tarantula crawling over her foot and had found a scorpion in her boot.

Harriet also met a kindred spirit in Belize.

> (If you've read *Anne of Green Gables*, you might remember red-headed Anne and her gushing about kindred spirits. Well, they exist. And Harriet met one of hers, a woman slowly dying of emphysema who lived in a tiny, decrepit shack on the western shore of the Sibun River
>
>> (the side that hardly anyone lives on)

with her husband.)

Harriet met this woman one day when she was with Wardell

(who now owns a house on Venice Beach)

and the hippy guy who was really terrific and whose name has been forgotten long ago, when the three were scouting locations for filming B-roll for the documentary *From Mayan Times to Citrus Times*, a project that dealt with the uses of the Sibun River by humans.

Wardell and the hippy guy who was really terrific and whose name has been forgotten long ago went with the kindred spirit's husband to look at his citrus groves, and Harriet stayed back to talk with her very new friend. Her very new friend made her some coffee, the awful instant kind that Harriet hates – Nescafe, but Harriet is polite and she had some with the woman. The woman's house is the kind of space that a writer who loved imagery and description could spend six pages on.

(We will be more concise: remember those old Sally Strothers commercials with flies landing on the faces of nearly starving children? This was one of those houses.

And, here was Harriet, sitting in it, drinking Nescafe with her new-found kindred.)

The woman asked Harriet for a cigarette, which was odd because archaeologists and anthropologists rarely smoke. But Harriet wasn't really either – she offered the woman one. And then, there they were in this shack, sitting on milk crates that had seen better days, and in fact had probably seen better decades, sharing coffee and cigarettes.

The woman brought up Monica Lewinsky. She spoke a Creole that Harriet had difficulty understanding, but Monica Lewinsky sounds the same in English or Creole, and Harriet recognized it. The woman told her it was a "shame, shame, shame" what was happening.

"Da man leds da contree, he sleep – or not sleep – ha, ha, ha! – wid whodeva he wants."

Harriet looked around the shack again. She saw a tiny television and remembered that all her kindred's husband had asked for from the *gringos* were batteries. She understood why. Here was her kindred living in a shack on the uninhabited shore; well, uninhabited except for her and her husband, of the Sibun River in central Belize with strong opinions about sexual freedom and the role of the private lives of public officials in the United States political arena.

This moment humbled Harriet more than the poverty of physical/material goods that surrounded her. Harriet before now had assumed that these "primitive peoples" knew little or nothing about her life, maybe as little or nothing as she had known about theirs. And, though this may be true – because her kindred had never experienced things like:

- Jumping into Lake Massapoag in Sharon, MA, at ten til eleven at night to wash off the sweat and chocolate sprinkles from a ten-hour shift of scooping ice cream before the police come and kick you and your fellow ice cream scoopers out,

- Telling a group of British tourists who are being given a historical and architectural tour by you at the Massachusetts State House all the awful things that happened between their county and yours on the lead up to your countries move towards independence,

- Experiencing your first kiss at the very old age of seventeen during the movie *Murder in the First* and having your first kiss last so long that strangers behind you threw gummy bears and popcorn at you, but even that not stopping the kiss,

- Skipping school and getting caught going to Walden Pond and then to the – now closed, however immortalized in the film *Good Will Hunting* – Tasty Diner, the one with the beautiful cook – the one who let you all eat for free the day Brenda did her Aretha Franklin impression so powerfully that you remember homeless men and Harvard professors staring from outside the window – instead of Religion, then Physics, then Calculus, then English class,

- Driving your Ford Fairmont station wagon, the one with the third gear "out of whack" that you always either had to double clutch or simply skip when accelerating to highway speeds-- the one with the trunk that never really closed again after the incident with the phone pole in the parking lot, from Boston to Connecticut the night you found out that one of your best friends had just lost her mother,

... We could go on for reams, but we won't. Instead – we will say that there was something beautiful in hearing this woman lecture Harriet about the Monica Lewinsky scandal. And, if this was an effect of globalization, Harriet didn't think it was necessarily bad. The two women discussed it – Harriet playing the role of the Puritan, talking about fidelity in marriage being akin to loyalty to government and dishonesty in one thing meaning the possibility for dishonesty in all things and *slippery slope* and *indiscretion* and *sex-crazed* rather than *focused on the job at hand*. The kindred spirit would hear none of it.

The two talked about life, love, and cooking.

>(This is the title of another book; one that hasn't been written. Not yet anyway.)

>The awful instant coffee cooled. The cigarettes burnt themselves out before really ever even being smoked at all. Two women on milk crates argued about blow jobs.

In other words, Harriet didn't think that the uber-sanitized trip that her boss had taken to Costa Rica was going to be very impressive. But, as a New-to-the-World-of-Offices Girl that she was, she listened, pretending to be attentive. Pretending to be attentive never stopped her from being "not hired."

2

(Harriet wasn't fired – she was merely "not hired."

>(America is funny when it comes to its corporate world euphemisms.

>It is somewhat entertaining that Harriet holds the paranoid belief that had she *not* mentioned to her boss

>>(who did research about health insurance policies

>>>(and was one of those Limousine Liberals that Harriet has come not to love))

>that she wanted health insurance *for herself*, she would not have been told that she was "not hired."

>>(There is a scene in the movie *Office Space* of which this episode reminded Harriet. Go see the movie yourself; this is a book, not a movie, and I'm not about to explain the movie to you.

(Sorry. This time it isn't sarcasm; it's plain ole nastiness, but remember – even narrators are human – unless of course they are omniscient, third-person narrators, in which case they are…)

Also, while you are at it, go see *Haiku Tunnel* and the British show *The Office*

(You probably already know the American version of that show.)

and you will laugh and know that Harriet feels she lived in these three productions whenever she worked in an office setting – which has been on and off for the past three years.[4] In fact, go see the following movies – that have nothing to do with the plot, or this tangent, at all –

Good Will Hunting
Solos
    (it is a Spanish film)
Say Anything
Amelie
    (a French one, but everyone already knows that)
In Juli
    (a German one)
To Have and Have Not

---

[4] In fact, Harriet is in an office right this minute. "How do I know that?" you ask. Don't. Curiosity killed the cat. "How?" you ask. Don't. I never did.

And I am still here to tell the tale –

the tale of a woman, yes, she is a woman, no matter how silly she may be and how much she loves to play with her four – no wait, he recently turned five – year-old nephew, ignoring the boring conversations of the so-called Adults – a woman who believed in love at first sight, until it happened to her.

The "real truth" is that Harriet's heart was not really broken. We just needed a plot, so we came up with that one. More women than men read fiction, and women tend to love that love crap. However, this is a men's book, but not many men will read it. It is a right-brain book written logically and tangentially, simultaneously. Sex sells as well, but there's little in this volume; we'll save that for the screenplay version.

In any case, right this minute, at 5:23 pm on Thursday, June 23, 2005, Harriet is sitting down on a blue chair with black, plastic armrests and is staring at the computer screen of a *Word* document. The computer screen is rather old; Harriet thinks she remembers the "I.T. Guy" telling her that it was nine years old when he came to do an inventory of the computer systems. She isn't positive of the age, but she does smile when she recalls that when the "I.T. Guy" came over on Tuesday afternoon to help her with a computer problem, he held out his hand, looked her straight in the eye, and said, "Hi, I'm Jay. I'll be your I.T. guy for the day..err..ummm...I mean week." She hoped that he was kidding. Not about being the "I.T. Guy," but rather about being so much of a dork.

Harriet, mind you, is a dork. A big one. A really big one. She loves dorks, but only the ones who are aware that they are dorks and are shameless about it, who intentionally say dorkish things to people who don't get it, just to be dorky. She hopes that the "I.T. guy" is a dork. The kind who knows it.

She is working for six days in an engineering/architectural firm over on East 45th Street between 2nd and 3rd on that island the Dutch got from the Native Americans for a mere twenty-four buckaroos – or so the story goes.

To protect the innocent – and the guilty – she won't give the exact address, but I have a hunch that it is on the 7th floor of 228 and that the company is called Highland Associates, but that is only a hunch.

In any case, Harriet is happy. She has one minute to go before she can leave for the day and actually doesn't hate the people in the office. One of them even invited her out for lunch this afternoon, though Harriet was hoping he would offer to pay, and he didn't, but he still was really nice to invite her.

Baraka

Before Sunrise and *Before Sunset*
    (but only if you like conversational-heavy flicks)

Napoleon Dynamite

The Misfits and *How to Marry a Millionaire*

The Cruise

The Killing of a Chinese Bookie

The Lady of Shanghai
    (or, *The Lady from Shanghai*. The Orson Welles film),

Harriet is back in the office. She has almost finished the water in her bluish-purple Nalgene bottle and has already finished her second cup of coffee of the day. One of the very few things that Harriet enjoys about being in an office – aside, of course, from getting paid – is the free coffee. Harriet likes coffee.

Harriet is in a good mood right now. Although she is really confused about whether or not to break up with her boyfriend – his name is Adel – we will get to him later; he isn't "the monk" – so we won't really "get to him" as he plays a minor, very minor, role in this story, Harriet is still in a good mood. As it is Friday, and she is well-rested and well-caffeinated, but not too much so, and as she has worked a full week and will get a paycheck large enough to pay her rent for the month, and as she has actually spent a pleasant week in this position, and as she has tentative plans to play *Risk* this evening with her boyfriend – his name is Adel but you should already know that, unless you have a really bad memory – you stupid pothead – or unless you decided at about page 7 not to try and remember everything in this text as it is so full of seemingly unrelated and useless bits of information, and as she is happy to be planning to clean and organize her share of the two-bedroom apartment she lives in, and as she has a photo show coming up in two weeks, a possible trip to Manomet, Massachusetts, next weekend for the 3rd of July, and a definite teaching-and-visiting-friends-and-the-countryside trip to England in less than one month, and as Harriet realizes all these things at this moment – she is in a good mood right now.

Harriet is both in an office and in a good mood. Those things do not frequently occur in tandem.

> *Battle of Algiers*
>> (a French film shot in a documentary style and extremely timely again, sadly, in this contemporary world of terrorism and fascism[5] and
>>> (a new version of)
>> colonialism)
>
> *Jersey Girl*
>> (the version from the 1980's)
>
> and
>
> *Beauty and the Beast*
>> (the Disney cartoon))

Yes, Harriet believed that she would have continued working there, indefinitely, without getting health insurance. She could be wrong.

> (She is wrong much more frequently than she would like to admit.))

Harriet's boss told this to her on the day that was also the last day of the bed sale. Harriet had promised the owner of the store that she would be in to make the deposit. She thought she was finished crying after three trips around the block, where paid gardeners looked

---

[5]The narrator is aware, as self-aware as an entity without a physical self can be, which is much more aware than one may initially think, much more aware in fact than many physical selves are, that the use of the word "fascist" is an opinion and a political one at that. The narrator is rather recalcitrant and is utterly unapologetic about this recalcitranism. The narrator is madly, deeply in love with the English language for many reasons – one is for its ability, at least in American-English, to grow new words whenever the occassion arises, *por emplo* "recalcitranism."

at her and smiled, trying to cheer up the young lady who was sobbing over a cigarette as she walked around the residential area just north of Geary.)

Back to G-d[6].

---

[6]It is illegal, or at least not permitted, to fall asleep while in the visitors' balcony of Congress. No, this has nothing to do with the main story.

Harriet was living in Washington, D.C., actually in Alexandria, Virginia, and she took a day trip with one of her best friends from college, Gloria, to visit the House and the Senate. Her friend, who is now a molecular biologist or geneticist, I'm not sure which, used to fall asleep all the time, while studying…at parties…in class…at work…in her car…all the time. She fell asleep in the visitors' balcony. Security made her wake up.

Our publisher wants Gloria to become more of a character; that is easy; Gloria is definitely a character. She and our heroine met many years ago in the *Howard Johnson* hotel when they were first moving into the dorm rooms on Commonwealth Avenue near Kenmore Square in September of 1996. Both young women were assigned to live in the hotel for the first semester of school, and both young women were from small towns and were terrified and excited to be living in the city and going to such a large, urban college.

Harriet saw Gloria, who reminded Harriet for some strange reason of a frog, and said, "Do you want to go to Burger King?" Gloria said yes. They were fast friends.

They shared memories – good, bad, and blurry – through the next four years of college and one summer in Chicago on a futon they had to share in Harriet's sister's tiny kitchen in Harriet's sister's tiny apartment in the "only bad part of the North Side of Chicago" where both slightly older young women took summer classes like the nerds they were (and are – Harriet argues, though Gloria would probably deny as she now lives in oh-so-hip Williamsburg with her artist boyfriend and buys clothes at places like Brooklyn Industry and Beacon's Closet and listens to cool music and knows all the bartenders at "The Abbey") and both slightly older young women worked as tour guides for Gray Line Trolley. They also had memories of the summer after college when seven ladies lived in a three-bedroom apartment in Alston and worked many hours and drank many beers and did not go to the beach or the library nearly enough.

(It seems to always come back to Him, doesn't it?)

They had many memories of living in San Francisco with four other friends from college in a lovely house on 9th Avenue in the Inner Sunset where the fog would roll in late afternoon and bury the house in white, wet air. They had several but not so many as many memories of Harriet's visits to Greenpoint, Brooklyn, when Harriet was trying to run around the world and would stop in Greenpoint and stay with Gloria in her tiny, but pretty, apartment on Newel Street.

3

He laughs at Harriet, but I think He likes her.

(G-d has a very perverse sense of humor. Sort of a cross

(No pun intended.)

between Edward Gorey

(who was not British – but has a sort of British sense of humor – and did all those weird cartoons for the beginning sequence of *Masterpiece Theatre*[7]),

Mr. Bean, and Monty Python.

(Yes, G-d does prefer British humour. He doesn't understand German humor, at all. And He gets embarrassed over the fact that

---

[7] *Masterpiece Theatre* is a mistake – this supposedly hot-shot narrator is indeed not always correct – Edward Gorey ought to be associated with *Mystery* and not *Masterpiece Theatre*. We apologize – we being the royal narrator and, if she was aware of this text, the fictional Harriet Zabrosky.

He does indeed tend to enjoy the crass, slapstick style of the Americans.

(G-d doesn't like to admit this either – but He really truly does love the Americans.

They are His favorite people.

It used to be the Israelites, but now it is the Americans.

He definitely, however, has never told them that.

Somehow, though, their leaders have often thought that – in fact, they went a step further – and claimed to be carrying out His mission...

G-d does not have a mission, and, if He did, He definitely would not ask the Americans to carry it out for Him.[8]

(They mess up everything.

(Okay, so that is not true. WWII. They didn't mess that up, however they did take a very long time to join in,

---

[8]Actually G-d does have a mission, indeed a very important one; why the heck would He have gone through all this beautiful trouble otherwise? The simplest word for it is *love* but the cooler, more energetic way of saying it is the Hebrew *tikkun olam*. Either way, we aren't even close. Too many of us aren't even trying. This really pisses G-d off, almost as much as when people cheat at cards or when they fart in a crowded subway car.

and most likely did so mainly because it looked to be profitable. In case you didn't know, it was. Europe was left a mess, the Russians only thought they knew what they were doing, the Japanese were broken and battered, Africa and Sud America didn't know they were capable of anything yet, but the good ole U.S. of A. was really born as a superpower when the war ended.

Try to argue with that.

I don't know much about history, but I do know that.

I also know that

- Morocco was the first country to recognize the United States as a country.

- Benjamin Franklin wanted the turkey to be named the national bird instead of the bald eagle.

- A descendant of the poet Matthew Arnold is now a writer living in London, and her name is Harriet Paige, and she is a fantastic cook[9]

(and a pretty decent writer, as well).

---

[9] Be careful when speaking Spanish to know the difference between *fantastic cook* and *fantastic pig*. Especially be careful of this if you are trying to compliment someone on her ability to cook well.

- The Pope John Paul II was also a poet and a playwright.

- *Evian* spelled backwards is naïve.

> (though I do know a fair bit about the post-colonial history of Sud America but only up to the first half of the last century with tidbits about Castro, Allende, and Peron thrown into the mix).

In any case, I am an all-knowing narrator

(and not Harriet)

(We both know very well that she is very far from being all-knowing.)

(Harriet herself knows that she is far from all-knowing.

> (Although, if the truth be told, and the truth ought to be told, always and everywhere, though it rarely ever is, and fiction is the BEST place to tell the truth.

The courtroom,

the newspapers,

the pulpit,

the soapbox,

the classroom,

the dinner table,

the bedroom

are all no places for the truth.

Bringing the truth there often leads to

jail,

lawsuits of libel,

excommunication,

condemnation, charges of heresy

riots, arrest, tar and feathering,

being placed on "unpaid academic leave,"

having your scholarship or funding "temporarily lifted,"

being grounded,

being threatened with divorce,

being forbidden to be affectionate in certain ways with your spouse that coming evening

as well as a host of other things:

being burnt at the stake, stabbed in the back, punched in the stomach

having your toes stepped on, your eyes deceived, your heart broken

accusations of perjury

being locked up in a sanatorium

having tomatoes thrown at you

being
disowned,
disinherited,

disenchanted,
dissed
and a slew of others beginning with "d-i-s."

No,

Keep the Truth in Fiction.

It's the only safe place for it.))))

4

For a novel that claims to not be political, there is a lot of America-bashing[10] going on.

In any case, don't be misled, both Harriet and myself, the all-knowing narrator, really, truly love America. Really, truly. I do because I am all-knowing, and I know that love is the most important thing to know, and the most important thing to do.

Harriet does because she has to. She is as American as apple pie and illegal wars in the name of democracy. She loves America because she is America. She loves herself, and you will love her too, just as you, too, love America.

---

[10]While on the topic of America-bashing, let's take a slight detour and spend some time asking some questions: America-bashing — what does it mean?

Who or what is America and how does one bash it??

Can Americans bash themselves and how do they do it?
Can non-Americans bash something they have never experienced and do not really know?

Is it inherent in the concept of America that it be allowed to not only be bashed, but to bash itself?

What does this have to do with Freedom Fries?

Was Janis Joplin correct when she sang, "Freedom is just another word for nothing left to lose"? Did Janis Joplin indeed give Leonard Cohen "head on the unmade bed," or is that simply a rumor, or is that simply Leonard Cohen being wishful in his song writing?

What does the freedom of speech have to do with America bashing?

And, finally, what is the political philosophy and/or ideology of

Harriet,
the narrator,
the author,
the publisher,
the leaser of the publishing house's office space,
the security guard in the lobby of the building of the publishing house's
       office space,
the person who empties the trash barrels after everyone else has left the
       publishing house's office space for the night,
the bookstore owner/sales clerk/librarian/teacher/friend who
       sold/lent/recommended this book to you,
the critic,
receptionist,
copywriter,
newspaper editor,
newspaper publisher,
UPS delivery man,
bookstore receiver,
library intern,
bookstore buyer?

What does someone's political ideology have to do with literature

You may think you don't love America

> (especially if you are German, French, or an anarchist studying Spanish in Guatemala),

but visit NYC, visit Queens, visit Astoria, in fact, visit 49th Street between 30th and 31st Avenue on a Sunday afternoon in late May, and you, too, will love America.

You will love the kids whose parents are born in over two dozen countries playing, fighting, laughing, and, on occasion, crying on the sidewalks as they play baseball, American football, "You are the monkey, and I am the zookeeper," or as they pat the new dog who moved in on the corner and who is a Boston terrier and is very cute, or as they scream and yell about the cat that crawled out the hole in the screen of the third floor apartment of the building three from the end on the west side of the street, or as they run to the ice-cream truck, or ride their bicycles and laugh at Harriet's new haircut.

You will listen to these kids, and you will love America.

You might not love the war in Iraq and a lot of other things, but these kids will make you love America.

Just as you don't love that Harriet always loses her keys or her cell phone, or that she always forgets which day your birthday is, or that she has already told you that particular story THREE TIMES BEFORE!, or that you were even there when that story was a live event and that she wasn't even there, and that you were the one who told her that story in the first place, or that Harriet says mean things a lot, especially when she is trying hard to be nice, you will love Harriet because Harriet loves you, and even though it is sometimes difficult to be around her for extended periods of time as she seems to move under a cloud of chaos and never take an umbrella, you will know that it really is impossible to not love someone who loves you as much as Harriet does. At first, it will be easy not to love her: she is flighty, forgetful; hell, she is a smoker, but — as the days and months and years go on, you will love her.

You will secretly, and sometimes not so secretly, root for her when she is attempting a silly battle for a silly reason. You will wish her well, and, if you can, you will help her out. You will know that you love her a lot, but that she makes you very tired, and you will wonder when she is going to

a) grow up,
b) settle down, and
c) be normal.

You know that she is already

a) grown up, that she was the most grown-up five-year-old that ever walked the halls of the J.H. Gibbons School.

You know that she is

b) settled in her heart, and no matter where she goes or what she does, she is settled in her heart, even if she doesn't realize this herself.

> (which she doesn't, but don't tell her. It keeps her motivated, and, plus, it is amusing to watch a woman so already settled in her heart go and look and try to find out how to settle her heart.)

c) Normal. What is normal? Define it, and I'll

let you know whether Harriet is or is not normal. I have a feeling she isn't and never will be, but I'll wait for your definition first. I'm in no rush: I'm all-knowing. Remember? I have no deadlines or fear of death, taxes, or any of that baloney that you mere mortals are stuck dealing with. I repeat: I am in no rush.))

But, this is not a political book. This is a novel,

a novel about

- stars in one's eyes
- hearts that get broken and
- heads that always have wheels turning,
  synapses firing, and
  conversational threads getting
  tangled, but
  never really understand what a
  soul is and
  how one got one to begin
  with and
  what one does when one
  does realize that one does have one.)

He would probably ask either the Canadians or the Icelandic people.

(Not, he repeats in the ears of the French and the Germans, and he whispers to the anarchist studying Spanish in Guatemala who will be too high to remember this in the morning, definitely not the Americans.)

However, He does like them. And, for the record, He was the one that spoke through Harriet that evening in Wedel, Germany, when she said that the "Americans love the best."

When the group of Germans that she was with tried to argue with Harriet's grand generalizations[11], God spoke through her again, "It is because Americans are so stupid."

This is true.
They are stupid.

---

[11]Harriet is often unapologetic about her grand generalizations. She likes to think life is a box with different-sized holes all over it and that part of life is the many shapes of things that you need to fit into the box using the different sized holes. Harriet realizes in reality that this is not true, however she enjoys making her grand generalizations – especially when they get people excited enough to argue with her about them. This may indeed be very immature of Harriet, but neither Harriet, nor I, the all-knowing narrator, ever claimed that she was mature. She, however, enjoys making people think. For this reason, she often intentionally makes ridiculous statements purely to get people thinking about why the statements are ridiculous.

5

No one knows this, but G-d does this, a lot, a helluva lot; He speaks through people. Harriet is in no way special. Well, Harriet is special but not special for the fact that G-d speaks through her. He speaks through everyone at some point or another, sometimes just to snort, because He finds that funny, but othertimes to try and make speeches about things that He knows He can't talk about anymore through burning bushes or clouds. He says a lot of really cool things, he writes a lot of R.E.M.'s lyrics and a lot of the stuff that they do on lounge radio is some more experimental transient kind of club music stuff that He has gotten into. He used to work with writers but no one reads anymore so he pretty much stopped.

(There is where the Elbe was at her elbow.[12])

---

[12] Harriet wrote a poem that includes that image of the Elbe at her elbow.

(The Elbe is a river, for those of you who haven't just googled it or who aren't very informed about the waterways of Western Europe.)

Elizabeth Dembrowsky

There is nothing so beautiful as an American woman with a college education and a credit card

Sarah Lee, Sarah Lee,
Lose me, Leave me
Alone and away from
The fat man quoting Nietzsche.
Germans on bicycles.
British boys on parade.
You and I drinking
Gay champagne.

He is like the rest
Who cook *pollo narango-chocolat*
Who brought bought chocolates
We never ate.
We eat everything –
Turkish sour milk –
Sour belly dancing
To 60's music.

The dj's always love us.
The men always leave us
Alone and away from
The fat man quoting Nietzsche.

The Elbe at our Elbow.
Baltic jellyfish- the drunk lecherous men
In liquid salted dirt.
Torpedoes and submarines-
No longer yellow-
Journalism a joke.
Journalists for fathers
In Oslo drinking colas
Not smoking cigarettes.

*The Pos*t apologies
For rushing the papers-
The release that never came
To Bible Belt boys and Muslim mums
Dead right. Dead wrong.
Leave it alone and away from
The fat men quoting Nietzsche.

I pour over the
Pores of the whores
Who haunt my dreams
Cousins lost forever smoking Pall Malls
Giving dirty looks from dirty jeans
To American men reading erotic magazines
Far and away from
Fat men quoting Nietzsche.

This is true. They are stupid.

(Harriet is one of these stupid Americans that G-d loves.

She has read many books, served for several years as a member of the debating team, and does well on those exams where you fill in circles with a pencil,

(which is why she tends to believe that the Foreign Service Exam graders do not always only mark essays on the principles of the writing rather than on the policies or opinions subscribed to within the text of the essays.

(In May of 2004 in London, two days after her passport was stolen, Harriet took her Foreign Service Exam,[13])

---

[13]In fact, Harriet had to sign a document that stated she would not reveal any of the information included on the test, so she won't. Instead, we will include a short fiction piece that Harriet wrote about a young woman suffering a mental breakdown during the period in which she was supposed to be taking the exam. For those of you who are a bit too literal-minded to understand nuance and such, let me be clear – the following work is FICTION.

Elizabeth Dembrowsky

Foreign Service Exam
WC: 3192

(WC is writer jargon for word count and is helpful for writers when they are looking at particular contests or magazines/websites/newspapers/etc. that have particular word count limits. In case you were wondering, this novel does not have a particular word limit.)

"Your government has been kind enough to provide you with pencils." The man laughed. Gloria stared up at him. Apparently, it was a joke. The room tittered nervously. Gloria didn't so much as smile.

The man continued in a voice of command and confidence, "Raise your hand if you need a pencil." With a nod, he sent his two assistants, both British, Gloria quickly noted, up and down the aisles of desks, handing out sharpened Number Twos to the irresponsible test takers that had come unprepared. Gloria assumed this was part of the exam. Who could be trusted to defend an embassy when they couldn't even manage to bring a fucking pencil to the test? Gloria stared with disdain at the rest of the people in the room. Most of them were younger, probably still in college. Probably – the sons and daughters of diplomats and professors, probably– Georgetown kids. She scanned the seven rows, looking for a kindred.

She found one in "The Loser." She knew before the exam began he would never make the cut, but she liked him nevertheless. She, at least, had bothered to come incognito – dressing the part in a smart skirt and Ann Taylor blouse. Even her shoes said Foreign Service – a pair of brown Clarks, functional enough to walk in for miles, but stylish enough to intimidate the Iraqi guards who would have no idea how to deal with a woman in power. She blended in here in London. It was easy.

The Loser was a sore thumb, and she was drawn to him for it. Short, spiky hair and a two-day unshaven look, the kid appeared ready to go spend the day in a music store, not at an embassy exam. He was reading. Already disobeying the rules: "Please only have a watch, a water bottle, Passport, and pencils on your desk. Everything else should be left at the front."

She pretended to rearrange her skirt and looked sideways down the row, trying to read the title of his book. *Fear and Loathing in Las Vegas.* Classic. She smiled. So maybe the C.I.A. could scoop him up as a spy, getting the low-down from stupid socialists in Hamburg or Berlin. He could take notes on anti-war organizations, finding activists that were naïvely playing into the hand of terrorists. Possibly, but a job with the Foreign Service was definitely not for this kid. What kind of respect could he command in Jordan? Who would listen to his Fourth of July speech in Albania? Gloria sat up straight and picked up her pencil.

She twisted it in her right hand, successfully managing "The Trick." In high school, the kids on the Debate Team had practiced it for hours: psyching out your opponent with a confident pencil twirl. Gloria smiled when she saw the Exam Moderator doing the same thing. They must teach it in the F.E. Gloria was in good company.

She glanced again around the room, noting that there were a few other "Adults" there. She knew none of them stood a chance. Well, yes, the online advertisement had listed ages 25-59 as appropriate for the positions, and she was well aware of the litany of Fair Employment Laws that had been added to the books since the Baby Boomers had begun aging, but she knew very well that not one of these "old folks" was getting in. Not with the stamina needed in the position these days.

What sort of an organization would hire someone who had lived through Vietnam? We need Patriots. We don't need historians. She wondered how the Foggy Bottom crowd would manage. Too many of them were Democrats, and the last thing the Administration was looking for these days would be another Clark or Kerry. They needed Neo-Con's, good ole boys, Bible Belt nationalists.

She wondered if being a New Englander would cross her off the list. The war for independence was started by her ancestors, and their roots were thick in the dirt of challenging authority. She wouldn't hire someone like her, for sure. But, then again, perhaps, to keep up appearances, hiring a Harvard girl would work in their favor. She could be a poster child for the Administration--someone who actually could read and speak articulately. A young, white Condoleezza.

She hoped so.

She glanced at her watch – 10:53. Seven more minutes of waiting. This was probably part of the exam, too; bureaucracy work and waiting go hand-in-hand. She knew, if they let her in, it would be the most difficult part for her; from birth she was impatient, sending her mother into the hospital two weeks early. The doctors nearly sent her mother home, until she practically delivered Gloria on the Emergency Room floor. Waiting was not her forte. She would have to learn.

She scanned the room again; The Loser was still reading. The first thing she would do when hired would be to fire the Exam Moderator. Rules are to be enforced or erased. What sort of precedent of obedience is commanded when you don't even have to obey a simple order of not reading a book at your desk? What sort of attentive employee was this? Another hack. A Georgetown grad with parents in well-placed positions. No wonder the terrorists were winning. This shmuck is one of our best and brightest? Yeah, right. Let's admit defeat now.

"Okay, well, I'm going to pass out the answer sheet first. Do not lift it up, do not turn it over. Keep it face down on your desk."

The two helpers scurried back to the podium and picked up their packages of cellophane-wrapped papers. The room was silent except for the competing sounds of plastic being torn and forced air being piped in from above. She listened to the whirl, thinking about how air conditioning and enforcing democracy were so closely linked. She imagined the Iraqi police sitting in stiflingly hot classrooms and knew that their learning curves would be a low riding asymptote. Remembering her U.N. internship to Kyoto, she thought of the Japanese ambassador lecturing on the import of a clean sterile working environment. Back then, in the nineties, the Japanese were still a viable economic threat. Sony and the technology scares. Buy American. She reached further back into her memory and recalled the P.S.A.'s sponsored by the American Cotton Growers Association; they had run a series of scare tactics as commercials – -a lower-income American mother and son packing up a shoddy house.

"Why do we have to move, Mom?" the boy whines.

"Because Daddy's company was closed, and he doesn't have a job anymore."

She lectures, staring down at her son, rubbing his head gently.

"But why did Daddy lose his job?"

"Because people aren't buying American-made products, Son."

She stares into the screen and hugs her boy closer.

"Americans are purchasing foreign goods, and there are very few manufacturing jobs for people like your father."

Sappy music plays. The image fades to black.

The series rivaled the fucking Communists, Gloria recollected. Propaganda, propaganda, all of it. She was glad to be able to finally get a chance to have her say. At least, my propaganda won't be so blatant. I'll either be upfront or extremely subtle.

Gloria had a plan, one she doubted anyone would agree with, but one that she was confident about: beat them to the punch of a boycott and simply return to isolationism. She wanted to place huge tariffs on any "cultural exports" and get militant about enforcing international property laws around the globe. Hire Gates' lawyers and make the U.S. a litigiously-based bargainer at the W.T.O. table.

They want Marilyn Monroe and Madonna – and to see our economy tank. Well, we'll take away their images of our beautiful women, take the movies from their shelves – unless they agree to pay up and pay well. Our economy can stand a five-year stint of economic isolationism. The prices of all those poor quality goods from China and Eastern Europe will rise with a tariff to outdo the Tea Tax, but Americans need to learn to appreciate quality and stop buying stupid crap. Why the hell would anyone buy that shit anyway?

Gloria knew better than to write that on her essays, she was well-prepared to give them exactly what they were looking for. She would write about the need for a cautious relationship with the Arab world, give a soft criticism of the

Bush Administration's push for enforcing democracy, quote from the failures in the E.U. and suggest a return to a concentration on domestic policy and a silencing of criticism from within. Give lip service to the Europeans, play it low in Israel, and let Bush's "Faith" be the excuse for the reversal.

"G-d spoke to me," she wrote the President's Radio Address in her head. "He told me peace is the way."

People would buy it--they like the guy. The Europeans would probably believe it as well, they would think the country crazy enough to actually base a foreign policy on the dyslexic rhetoric of a self-appointed prophet of Christ who could be also capable of flip-flopping on such important issues.

Religion isn't an opiate – it's a spur. With the right spin, it can work wonders. Gloria smiled thinking about the five-year plan she had laid out for herself.

First, she had to pass the exam. She wondered what would happen if she didn't. Almost any job these days was tied to either defense contracts or some form of security. Maybe she ought to have listened to her father and stayed in the protected towers of academia. But, even there, things had changed. A slew of the East Coast colleges had been taken over by corporate-minded conservatives in the early 90's, and the days of open dialogue, a relaxed atmosphere, or any form of political activism were long gone. The 60's and 70's were a faraway memory, and, furthermore, someone like Gloria would not have been a ripe recruit. Cynical and cautious, Gloria was not someone drawn to anything as idealistic and irrational as the hippies. Free love and acid were not things that would have tempted her.

Working for the embassy would be her way out of the provincialism of Maine and a way for her to use her analytical skills in the service of the state. Yeah, right! Gloria didn't take a minor in history to not know that civil service was about as noble as being a slumlord. Those days had passed even before Vietnam.

The job would be just that – a job. The world had become a closed place after 9-11. The U.S. government seemed adamant: either participate in the war against terrorism or step aside.

America had lost before it had even entered.

The instructor started reading a script of instructions. Gloria began filling in the circles on the exam sheet. Name, Last. Name, First. Date of Birth. Place of Birth. Social Security Number. Address, Permanent. Address, Abroad. Sex. Weight. Height.

She filled in the form quickly, tapped her pencil down on the desk, and looked up. The Exam Moderator was staring at her. She smiled at the man. He didn't smile back. He simply looked back down at his script and read, "Now," he paused, "fill in your first name in the space marked Name, First."

Shit! Already her impatience was getting her into trouble. She slowly traced each circle a second time, pretending to be following along with the others.

When the Exam Moderator actually gave instructions for the exam to begin, Gloria was on the verge of a nervous breakdown. Sitting and waiting made her that way. She tore open the exam cover and began. A rush of adrenaline flowed through her. Exams were like drugs for Gloria. Ever since grade school, it had been that way. Other girls would get themselves sick and/or pee themselves in anxiety before Spelling Tests; Gloria would wait impatiently, anxious to have to try and prove herself. She and her mind had been at war with the world since age seven. She never needed friends, merely looked for subjects or nemeses. Either control them or fight them – she was a born leader.

The first question was:

Which of the following individuals won the Nobel Prize for Literature:

a) Che Guevara
b) Pablo Sanchez
c) Gabriel Garcia Marquez
d) Isabel Allende

Gloria nearly laughed. Che Guevara! *The Art of Motorcycle Maintenance and Guerilla Warfare* would have been a great book. She knew straight off that it was Marquez; she hated his books, but had to read them in high school for a World Lit Class. What she was unsure of was why exactly literature from South America had any bearing on her ability to serve her country. This test was strange from the start.

Question two read:

In order to stay positive when discussing a subordinate's work performance, one should:

a) lie and make the worker feel better.
b) mention only negative tasks so the worker would not then ask for a raise.
c) first give a positive overview of worker's performance and then remind the worker of areas that need improvement.
d) give the worker a paper report and refuse to discuss the contents.

Gloria looked around the room. What sort of a test was this? Management skills? She thought the exam was about history and background knowledge. Skills about working under pressure and analytical abilities. Not about how well one can handhold an employee. She reread the list and penciled in c. She knew that d would be the only thing she would actually ever do, but realized that the analysts wanted c. She could give them what they wanted--for now.

The third question read:

In the nineteen-nineties, national history curriculum underwent a drastic swing to the left. Revisionist historians and ultra-liberal academics influenced much of the educational track of young people in America. This resulted most dramatically in:

a) a rise in registered Republicans among young people as students quickly recognized they were the victims of propaganda from the left.
b) a rise in registered Democrats among young people as students fell victim to the biased information.
c) a refusal of young people to take part in the political process at all on account of the liberal education system that had taught them that all politics were corrupt.
d) a dumbing down of education.

Gloria couldn't believe her eyes. What the hell was this question? She had been educated under this system and had read Chomsky and Zinn. She was familiar with Michael Moore and the arguments made by these Americans against U.S. foreign policy. She knew about the School of the Americas and about the C.I.A.'s covert dealings in Latin America. She hadn't considered any of those readings as causing any sort of "dumbing down." In fact, she thought herself lucky to have been able to have had access to more of the truth about her nation's actions. In fact, it was part of the reason why she was applying with the Foreign Service anyway; she was looking to take an active role in stopping what she feared was her country's highway to hell.

She reread the question. Not one of the answers provided her with any reasonable answer. She realized that the answer had to be either a or b only because one of the partisan voting numbers had to have altered, but then again, she remembered her logic class in college and realized that correlation does not equate causation. D definitely could not have been the answer; it was too blatantly flippant. She reread c and thought about her peers. Most of them didn't vote. Even the "activist" ones didn't – accusing the entire system of being corrupt and deciding to take local action rather than participate in the federal process that the 2000 Elections had shown was a sham.

But she didn't think the creators of the test agreed with what she knew from firsthand experience. She left the answer blank and continued to the next question.

The following musician wrote the song "Blowin' in the Wind":

a) Bob Dylan
b) Peter Seeger
c) Woody Guthrie
d) Joan Baez

What did this have to do with the war in Iraq? Gloria was outraged at the exam. She knew the answer was Dylan and that Baez had made the song popular during the Vietnam War as a protest song, but couldn't find it to be at all relevant to her ability to represent the U.S. government in foreign countries. What the hell was this exam about?

She remembered seeing a postcard in City Lights bookstore in San Francisco. The haven for the Beatnik writers of the 50's and the 60's. She remembered the postcard that she almost purchased at the checkout counter. It was a black and white photograph taken of recruits at West Point. The full class was reading Allen Ginsberg's *Howl*. She remembered laughing then – the military's attempt to know their enemy – poets. It wasn't so funny anymore.

Gloria started to lose her ability to concentrate. It was a first for her on any exam. She never panicked, but right now sweat was starting to form beads on her forehead. She wiped them away and left the question blank, forgetting to fill in the circle for a.

She flipped through the exam and saw dozens more questions. She read them quickly and found more and more propaganda. She looked around the room--was anyone else aware of the lunacy of this test? The room was full of busy test-takers working away, eyes focused on their test booklets. She returned to her own booklet and flipped through it again. She started to lose her ability to even read the questions. Tears filled her eyes. What was happening to her? She was sweating profusely by now. Her left leg had started shaking. She looked at the exam administrator; he was staring at her.

Suddenly, as if a force beyond her control had taken over, she threw her exam off her desk and stood up.

"Bullshit!" she yelled, surprised at her own outburst.

The entire room looked at her – except for The Loser; he kept working away.

The Exam Moderator walked towards her. The two assistants stood back, staring blankly at her. She looked at the others in the room.

"Bullshit!" she yelled again. "This is fucking bullshit!" She thought she saw a pitying look from one of the older test takers that she had been mentally mocking earlier. She walked calmly to the front of the room and picked up her bag. She looked at the Moderator whose mouth had opened as if he was about to speak.

She smiled at him, and said it for the third time. "Bullshit!" She left the exam and ran down the two flights of the stairs. She pushed open the door and ran out into the unseasonably warm London air.

Harriet truly believes that her essays against enforcing democracy across the world and concerning both the ironic stupidity and moral laziness in giving up civil liberties to protect the "land of the free" were very well argued.

She tends to think that the exam evaluators are indeed looking for opinions that match their policies.

Harriet thinks that diversity in opinion makes democracy grand – she thinks groupthink is dangerous and does not like the idea of her government being run by people who all agree with one another.

> (Harriet especially espouses this belief when these people agree with each other and not with her.

Harriet

> (as with most human beings)

likes to think of herself as correct.

(However, even Harriet can have enough anti-hubris to admit that she

> (unlike some other individuals who share this cute, little planet with her)

is not infallible

> (in regards to issues of faith or about the weather),

she continues to feel very strongly about the misuse of Christianity by the Christian Right.

> (No, you aren't about to read about the monk yet, but the time will come, please be patient.

My Monk

There will,
however, be a
brief reference
— but it will be
fleeting

> (as is
> the
> case
> with
> most
> refer-
> ences))

(Harriet, according to
the monk, is like most
women

> (Harriet found
> the monk to be
> very sexist.)

in that she is "terrifying
with all those purpose-
less emotions."

> (The monk
> wrote that in a
> poem —

(A poem Harriet likes to think refers to her.)

(The monk was a poet.

He was a trained economist as well.

He is also from Romania.))

Now is not the time to read about the monk.)

Harriet is very much opposed to people starting wars in the name of Christianity

(she thinks they are missing the point)

or democracy.).))

but Harriet is still very stupid. In fact, she is one of the most stupid of all Americans.

Harriet is **_Intentionally Naïve_**

>(but really this is a shoddy mask for her cynicism

>>(Harriet is very cynical.

>>>(Harriet smiles a hell of a lot for a cynical person.)).))

G-d knows this, but still likes them.

Sometimes the smart ones are so boring,

and the smart ones almost never believe.)))

7

She is definitely not as good as she would like to think she is. She is actually mean and manipulative, but tries to keep that in check.

(Harriet tries to keep this in check by dwelling on other people's criticisms of her. Not everyone – just the people she cares about. This seems nice and genuine; however, it is frustrating to be friends with Harriet because if you criticize her actions, she expects a full thesis on the moral implications of what she has done wrong and how she ought to improve. Some of her friends would like it if she took life less seriously. Others think she should take it more seriously. Harriet isn't sure who is right, but is either very serious or very non-serious all the time. She rarely just is

(except when she is sleeping.

Sleeping is when Harriet has wonderfully boring dreams.

Nothing exciting whatsoever – just mundane, day-to-day actions. Harriet loves her dreams.

(It is the awake thoughts that tend to worry her so much. But she puts her trust in them —

well, she doesn't know where she puts her trust — but she continues to get out of bed in the morning.

(Well, she continues to get out of bed on most mornings.

Occasionally, she waits until the afternoon.

(She feels very guilty[14] when she does this.)))).

She wishes she could shut off the monkey-brain more often, but has difficulty.

(She also drinks a lot of coffee; this could have some effect on thinking, but she continues to drink coffee. She went to see a doctor once about the amount of coffee she drank but he told her as long as she was okay with the digestion reaction there was nothing to worry about — no ulcers from coffee. She kept drinking coffee, this time with a clearer conscious.

---

[14] Guilt. Harriet's mother hates that Harriet feels this way and says, "My mother was a Protestant; I was never raised with it, and NEITHER were you" whenever Harriet talks about the degree to which she feels burdened with Catholic guilt, even though she is no longer a Catholic.

Her father once said, "Once a Catholic, always a Catholic." Harriet didn't like that, but sometimes thinks that maybe he was right. It is VERY annoying!

(She actually likes the inability to shut off the monkey-brain[15]

(except on occasions late at night, when she has something important to do in the morning)).

She also drinks tea.

(She picked up this habit after living in England and being told that tea has more caffeine in it than coffee.

(Harriet does not believe that tea has more caffeine than coffee, but does appreciate that tea is gentler on her stomach than coffee.

(Harriet has a very bad stomach.)

Harriet also believes that everyone is lying at all times.

For someone who chooses to be **Intentionally Naïve**, thinking that everyone is lying at all times is a strange trait to possess.

---

[15]Oh, yes, *monkey-brain*. I guess you want a definition of that – it is a term that Harriet's favorite aunt coined; a description that is supposed to probably be the *monkey-in-your-brain* running around like crazy and never stopping to rest on one particular idea for a very long time. People could say that this is Attention Deficit Disorder – but I like to call it the *monkey-brain*.

My Monk

Harriet doesn't necessarily believe that people are always trying to lie –

rather,

she feels that

tomfoolery

ballyhoo

shenanigans

ignorance

and

outright bullshit[16]

---

[16]There is a grand book – actually, it is more like a pamphlet although it is sold and packaged as a book (even more bullshit), called *On Bullshit*, written by some adorable academic who was interviewed on Jon Stewart's television program, *The Daily Show*. Harriet does not like television, but her roommate introduced her to the show, and she found the satire smart and witty – as all satire should be. Recently, she has been way too busy to watch the show, but has enjoyed the few episodes she has seen, including the one where the author was interviewed. She does not remember his name and is not right now in New York City with her roommate and so can neither ask her roommate if she remembers nor go to the local bar and ask the dj or his girlfriend if they could please give her back her copy of *On Bullshit* so that she can look at the author's name.

No, Harriet is not in Astoria, Queens; she is in Oak Bluffs, Martha's Vineyard. This will make sense later; well, it will make sense later to an extremely

account for a good number of these falsehoods being shared amongst the conversing inhabitants of this cute, little planet Earth.

She is so convinced of this that she waits until an individual says the same thing for a second time before she listens to him or her.

astute reader, but true to form, or true at least to Harriet's paranoid impulses – Stanley Moss did decide to let her go before giving her health care. He told her that he is hiring his son for her position, which Harriet "thinks" is a lie, but is not fully sure; sometimes her paranoid impulses are just that and are completely unfounded. And, as Harriet wishes not to be sued for libel, she better be sure to only mention that she "thinks" something because although this is a novel, it is a true novel, and one can never be too careful.

In case you are confused, maybe the following will help:

The fact that Harriet "thinks" something in the above instance is her own way of self-protection. She is not quite bullshitting when she uses the term "thinks". Rather, she is "covering her own ass". Unfortunately, in contemporary American culture, this is very important to do. Some people are so good at both bullshitting and covering their own ass that they rise quickly to the top and few people notice. Harriet finds this phenomenon most interesting when the risers themselves do not notice.

However, Harriet is without work come next Monday morning. She is not worried though. However, her mother is. However, her father is not. In fact, he thinks that the fact that Harriet thinks she can write a play in one week, which is what Harriet is planning to do, that's why she gave herself the excuse that she could go to Martha's Vineyard for the week even though when she gets back to NYC there will be no job, but a lot of bills waiting for her, is very impressive, or at least very ambitious.

By the way – this play will go on to be written, it will be "work- shopped" over a period of several months by the Naked Artist Collaborative, directed and produced by Lovecreek Productions and later by White Trash Intellectuals Productions and will be nominated, submitted, accepted, and performed for/to/by/at the Samuel French Festival – however it will not win and it will not be published under the name of Harriet Zabrosky. How do I know this – I just do.

My Monk

Her theory is as follows:

If someone repeats his or her lie, he or she may actually believe it. Or at least, it was not a passing thought floating through the individual's head that he or she[17] decides to utter out loud

      (as is the case with almost everything people

          (especially Americans

              (and, according to the monk, most women))

      say).

---

[17]Being POLITICALLY CORRECT can make for very cumbersomely structured sentences, but, ehhh, Third Wave Feminists have been lax thus far on re-reinventing the grammar rules.

There is a possibility that the passing thought may float through the said individual's head twice; however, Harriet believes that the chance of this occurring is statistically insignificant and still keeps her practice of waiting for someone to repeat their factoid twice before letting her mind hold it in its stored memory.

Furthermore, she believes that if someone says the factoid twice, he or she may even believe his or her lie, in which case, she tries to compare this factoid with others filed in her brain and decide whether to ultimately put the factoid in the category of:

Said Individual believes this to be true and is most likely correct

or

Said Individual believes this to be true and is an idiot because this is not at all true.

Harriet has no category in her brain for:

Said Individual believes this to be true and is completely correct.

Harriet forgets much of the information regarding the

Null Hypothesis

and such; however, she thinks it is somehow related to her theory that there are no known truths, only known non-truths.

She would have to ask Gloria, the chemist, geneticist, molecular biologist, or whatever it is that she is, but would rather talk to her about:

- their dead-end jobs,

- men, and

- how happy they are to both be living in New York City even if they:

- hardly ever see one another,

- are very poor,

- and have very long commutes to and from work everyday[18]

---

[18]Actually, Harriet does not have a very long commute to and from work everyday as she is unemployed. She was, however, employed for many weeks up in

Riverdale in the Bronx, at which time she did indeed have a very long commute to and from work everyday. Perhaps, it was this particular commute that Harriet would refer to when she and Gloria would speak.

Although Harriet remains unemployed, she still gets work from time to time from the staffing agencies that she has contacted. Her most recent and favorite position was as the Executive Assistant for the CFO of the United Jewish Communities. Even though Harriet is a goy, no one seemed to treat her differently at the position. In fact, the COO/CFO of the company was very nice to her – in fact, he offered her a peach from his lunch; in fact, he even knew her name after only being told it once. In fact, he was the nicest two-day boss that Harriet has ever had.

Actually, actually, Harriet is currently employed. She is right now temping at the United Jewish Communities, where the security is depressingly stringent – depressing as it is such a sad commentary on contemporary life…in any case, Harriet somehow got a gig helping to organize the "GA" which is short for General Assembly, which is sort of like the UN or G8 of the Jewish organizations around the world – well, except that votes aren't taken – or at least Harriet doesn't think so. In any case, she is no longer working for her favorite two-day boss, but instead is working for several women, none of whom appear to be in charge, but all of whom appear to want to be. There is a woman named Karen who works next to her, who is nice, and possibly Jamaican, or at least, some sort of Caribbean something or other. Karen moves slowly and is very kind – Harriet has a non-sexual crush on Karen, but probably would end her crush if she really needed to use the copy machine and Karen was in front of her in line.

On the other side of Harriet is a wall; Harriet likes the wall. It makes her feel more like she is in an office and less as if she is in a cubicle. Behind the wall is a woman named something that Harriet has forgotten, but hopes to remember within the next 33 minutes, so that when she leaves for the night, she can walk by this woman, give her a brief, half-wave, and a smile and say, "Goodnight,-------."

On the other side of this name-unknown woman is another woman named Karen, which makes things a bit difficult. Harriet has already messed up three people's names by putting different first names with different last names – a lot of these names seem the same to her. Which is sort of funny, because when one of the women who appears to want to be in charge introduced Harriet to the members of a meeting – those in the room and those over the phone – she

My Monk

(If you, however, care enough to know for sure, go grab a high school science teacher and ask for a full explanation of it.).))))

pronounced Harriet's name strangely and then paused dramatically and asked, "Is that the correct pronunciation?" Harriet smiled because she thinks that her name is pretty easy to pronounce, but Harriet would think that because Harriet has lived with this name her whole life.

As we are on the topic of Harriet's work schedule, she was in a position last week and the week before that with a group of people that she really liked – she isn't sure why she liked them, but she did. Maybe it was because on the first day of the job the head of the admin staff bought pizza and on the second day during a lunch meeting, they ate Cuban food, and then on her last day, one of the Project Managers brought in grapes and cookies and bread and cheese and salami. There was also free coffee, ALL DAY LONG, at this job. Harriet liked this job so much, or rather, she liked the particular office perks, that she got special permission to stay late and work on her own writing projects. She would sit at the computer and type and edit and occasionally send emails to her friends. Harriet would actually like to write an entire novel while in offices in New York City – but prefer that she would first secure health care and a boyfriend.

Oh yes, by the way, Harriet did end up deciding to break up with Adel for reasons too personal and too difficult to mention. The "love story" of this book is not the Moroccan, but the Romanian.

8

She wants to be a writer to satisfy this *monkey-brain* of hers, but so far has only been able to write short stories.

(She has written over two hundred pages of short stories.).

She also wrote travelogues, one collection of very funny stories about childhood, several childrens stories, three plays, four french hens, and has kept dozens of diaries over the years.

She wrote 75,000 words of a novel, but decided instead to write it as a screenplay. She finished the screenplay, but her 'agent'[19] found it too literary and the characters too intellectual. This was very frustrating for Harriet.

---

[19]Harriet actually does have an 'agent.' Surprised? She is too. And not only that, so is her publisher. Thing is, the 'agent' is simply a nice woman who lives in way-western Mass and who reads everything that Harriet sends to her, usually sending it back with a nice little note explaining why she isn't interested in shopping it. However, she is interested in Harriet's screenplay *Matilda- All Grown Up* which is the precise reason why Harriet cannot seem to finish the screenplay and instead is writing "other" things.

(Harriet is now trying to get a job in advertising.[20]

    (She hopes the work will help her to be less literary and less intellectual.

        (Harriet doesn't think that someone who spells as poorly as she does can be really considered an intellectual. She also does not consider herself literary; at most she likes to think that she may be well-read, but after living in England for a year, she decided that she is not well-read either.)))

Harriet writes poetry also, but she is trying to stop.

---

[20] By the way, the advertising gig fell through. The interviewer, and owner of the company, was very nice and told her to stay in touch or something to that effect, but did not hire her, which could be just as well: Harriet working everyday on the sixty-something'ith floor near Penn Station could have been a disaster.

Harriet might very well go back to writing poetry. Well, especially if she lands a grant from the Grub Street Press in Somerville, MA. They are looking to give $2500 for 50-75 pages of great poetry work. Harriet would like to think she has that – but she is not a member of any elite set and so does not really know what they are looking for. But, she knows what she is doing

    (in her writing, not in her personal life)

and hopes that someone, somewhere, will get it.

Actually, she hopes to be Yoko Ono and find her John Lennon. Do you know that story? He attended her art opening; she had a step ladder that led to a tiny word on the ceiling with a magnifying glass attached to it wth a string. Lennon climbed the ladder, read the word, 'yes,' and said yes to her.

She wants to write poetry when she is famous or rich or rich and famous. She does not want to write poetry when she does not have health care or a steady paycheck.

She likes to think she is similar to Dostoyevsky's Prince

(in the book *The Idiot*)

(Harriet likes to use the phrase "smiling like an idiot."

(The monk used it first, in describing walking around the hills of Devon, England, and Harriet liked it and adopted it.)

(In fact, Harriet likes the phrase so much that one day she would like to write the story of her life and call it *Smiling Like an Idiot*. However, Harriet feels strongly that writing the story of one's life is a pretty conceited thing to do – and she doesn't really plan to do it, but sometimes she sits and thinks about titles of this book she never plans to write.

Other titles include, but are not limited to:

Devastatingly Single
How to Avoid A Steady Paycheck and Health Care
I'd Sell-Out If Anyone Was Buying
An Overachieving Slacker

Coffee and Cigarettes

>(though Harriet knows that this particular one is also the title on an independent film. She knows this because she actually saw this independent film, while in Hamburg, Germany, no less; hmmm, for a constantly broke girl, she gets around. She remembers the title of the film because she liked the film. She remembers laughing out loud – louder than anyone in the theatre, several times. She thinks this was because some of the references were for an American-mind. She isn't positive, but she does remember Tom Waits telling Iggy Pop that the coffee at IHOP was very good. Harriet laughed and laughed and laughed at that part. No one else in the theatre did.)

>*Everything I Ever Needed to Know I Never Learned The Bohemian Capitalist.*)),

minus the epilepsy and the wealth.

She read that story when she was staying in Birmingham,

>(U.K., not Alabama)

with Kate DeRight and Paul Something-or-other[21].

Elizabeth Dembrowsky

She had said goodbye to the monk

(Yes, we will get back to him.)

a month or so earlier and was reading the great Russian writer as a way to keep the memory of the monk active within her.

(Harriet is not very good at letting go.

    (Her best friend of over twenty years

        (Harriet turned 27 in February

            (and was very sad that the monk did not write to acknowledge her birthday).)

    is the person on the planet that knows her the best and fights with her the most. Though, now that they are both adults,

        (Harriet's best friend is now married and recently bought the house she was raised in from her parents.

        (Harriet was the maid of honor

---

[21]Paul Something-or-other is in a band called Narondni Trida that pretends to be a band from the Czech Republic when in fact they are really a band from in, and around, Birmingham, England. Narondni Trida entitled their first album *Exhibitionism* in honor of a photo show that Harriet held at the University of Warwick.

(and thought that her dress made her look like a banana even though everyone said she looked nice)

and got to give a speech.

(It was a short one

(much shorter than the one that the best man, Michael Mussman, gave. Much better too, Harriet thought, but knew that the best man had written his down on a piece of a paper.

(Harriet made up her speech as she spoke.

(Though, Harriet later learned that her best friend didn't fully appreciate her fly-by-the-cuff method of working even if she was okay with the final product.))).)

She spoke about commitment in uncertain times and made people cry. She loves her best friend of over twenty years

(a lot) –

so much so that she has to tell her that all the time.

Harriet would like to think that her best friend likes to hear it and doesn't get annoyed.))

they fight much less frequently.)

Once Harriet makes a friend, she tends to hold on. She was friends with the monk that she fell in love with and is very confused about staying his friend.)

She had read *Crime and Punishment* in college and later had also read *Notes From the Underground* and loved them both, although she was terrified by the effect that *Crime and Punishment* had on her. She read it at the request of a cute, Russian-born business student from Staten Island.[22]

---

[22]He is married now. Or, at least, that is according to the last Harriet has heard about his plans.

She had a crush on him at the time, her second year in college, and had agreed to read the "best book ever written." Although, in the end, she didn't agree with his assessment, she was "greatly moved" by the work. For the first, actually second, time she felt capable of murder.[23]

Harriet did have him over for Easter one year – it was his first, and probably last, Easter with a half dozen other vagabonds from college. And she did drive through Buffalo and stop in and visit him when he was in law school. And she did meet up with him and two other college friends at some trendy restaurant in NYC. And she remembers hearing that he was a lawyer working for "The City" and was engaged to another lawyer. She thought of the privileged kids he would have and was happy to think he had gotten what he wanted from the American Dream – even if it hadn't been her.

Actually – she now knows this for sure and met his wife – who she likes a lot because his wife is just as smart as he is (if not more so) and makes great desserts and agreed to be photographed at eight months pregnant with him for a photo project called People Not Smiling in Their Own Homes even though she smiled a lot during the photo shoot and now is a proud mom of a sweet baby girl.

[23]The first time was in church. On Good Friday, she would have to go to service where the Passion was read. She hated having to do it, but she would have to recite the lines "Crucify him, Crucify him," with the rest of the parish. She now thinks it was a mean trick of forcing guilt on the parishioners, but she remembers getting teary-eyed and thinking how awful it was to crucify Jesus, "because he was G-d and everything." She would whisper "don't" before the line, as if that would change things. She used to cry at that part of the service. Nowadays, she cries at the following: old couples holding hands, babies laughing, strangers giving up their seats on the subway. However, those Good Fridays made her feel as if she too were a murderer.

She also cries when her heart gets broken or when she is very angry and wants to yell but doesn't. She also cries at other things too, but nothing all that interesting, idiosyncratic, or noteworthy.

She doesn't cry at the reciting of the Passion – though she did cry during Mel Gibson's film whenever the actress that played Mary appeared. Harriet is not a mother, but she would like to be one, one day, and she wouldn't want her son to be crucified. This is why she is adamantly against the death penalty.

Elizabeth Dembrowsky

She, at this time in her life, was an aspiring pacifist.

(She continues to be an aspiring pacifist

(which is part of why she was afraid to move to New York.

(Harriet thought that it would be very difficult to be an aspiring pacifist in a city like New York.

The death penalty is one of many reasons why she is very, very frustrated with her government.

She does really, in her deepest heart of hearts, love America – her life would be so empty without sweet and sour sauce on French Fries and the music of R.E.M. Hell, she wouldn't be alive if it wasn't for America – this country made her.

However, this does not stop her from sometimes getting mad at her great-grandparents – wishing they had stayed in Europe so that she could have been "sophisticated."

But then she quickly comes to realize one of two things would have happened if they had stayed in Europe:

1. Her Spanish great-grandmother and her French great-grandmother would never have become pregnant with children that would have met at a beach before the beginning of World War II. And then, her mother would never have been born and never would have met that man driving that convertible car on Cape Cod and then things would have been completely different.

2. If her Polish relatives had stayed in Poland – they would not be the cosmopolitan elites at the "oh-so-hip" dance clubs in Krakow that Harriet saw when she went there. They would be out in the country, where some of them still live, farming potatoes and barely even knowing that Communism had ended fifteen years previously.

(Harriet has only been in New York for a little over three weeks, but finds that it is neither easier nor more difficult than anywhere else.

(Being an aspiring pacifist is very hard--anywhere. It is especially hard when people get angry when you tell them that you are an aspiring pacifist.

(Harriet has always found that odd.

9

Who cares if someone is an aspiring pacifist?

Really, Harriet thinks, *the world would be a much better place if there were more aspiring pacifists – maybe a little bit more crowded, but, still, a much better place.*))))))

She was also scared of how expensive New York was

(but New York is actually less expensive than England

(especially when you agree not to go out drinking on weeknights when you don't have a job, and especially when you live off of:

- coffee,
- cigarettes, and
- pasta

(though – cigarettes in NYC are very, very expensive.))).

The third thing she was afraid of was being lonely.

A good friend who moved to New York City immediately after graduation from college had told her "New York could be the loneliest place on the earth."[24]

(The good friend was one of the most outgoing and gregarious of all of Harriet's friends

(her name is Erica, by the way)

(and Harriet has a lot of outgoing and gregarious friends).)

Leonard Cohen

(one of Harriet's favorite "contemporary poets")

sings, "New York is cold, but I like where I'm living."

(Harriet is pretty confident that "cold" refers to more than simply the temperature.)

---

[24]And, faithful reader, it can be. Oh, yes, it can be.

But, so far, the city was not lonely at all. In fact, Harriet thought it was very friendly.

(She theorized that 9-11 changed the city for the better in that sense. She never remembered NYC being so friendly when she was younger.

(She used to come to visit her aunt in the Bronx and in college made trips to Manhattan for middle of the night visits to Times Square

(solely so that she could stand and stare at the bright lights and then get back into a car and drive back to Boston in time to get to class in the morning),

and she would visit her friend Dat [pronounced *dot*] the aspiring filmmaker who now lives in Washington, D.C. with his wife Kat, in "oh-so-hip" Williamsburg))

In three short weeks, she had already experienced several examples of this uplifted, friendlier NYC:

1. Her landlady's sister remembers her name after only being told it once. Her landlady's sister also picked up and saved a computer plug that Harriet had dropped when she was moving in.

(Unfortunately, her landlady's sister did not find the wallet of Harriet's that was lost during the move.

> (G-d denies being involved in this particular case of the lost wallet.
>
> He laughs at the incident, but continues to claim He was not involved.
>
> He finds it funny, that even when He leaves her alone, she still seems to lose her wallet.))

2. People make eye contact.

(Harriet thinks even more so than in the suburbs.

> (Harriet lived in the suburbs of Boston prior to moving to New York City.)
>
> (Harriet was raised in the suburbs of Boston.))

3. Subway courtesy is more prevalent in NYC than on any of the public transits that Harriet has ever been on.

(Harriet has been on public transit systems in the following cities:

Boston
Chicago

Washington, D.C.
San Francisco
Philadelphia
Barcelona
Warsaw
London
Hamburg
Strasbourg
Paris
Berlin
Birmingham

    (U.K., not AL)

    (The nicest thing that happened to Harriet

        (so far)

on the public transit system in New York City happened when she on her way to the interview for the position in advertising

    (See? The tangents

        (sometimes)

    come full circle

(in case you are lost, a reference to a position in advertising was made several pages ago.

I'm not going to tell you which page, because the pagination will surely change. But the footnote is number 20, and Harriet's roommate, a very nice person, works in publishing

(for an academic press);

don't worry, Harriet has little-to-no contacts in the literary fiction world and will have a

very,
very,
very

difficult time getting this manuscript published.

She continues, however, to have an idiotic level of optimism that things will work out in the end even if she keeps to her ideals

and remains fixed on her goals –
a

very,
very,
very

difficult task as Harriet alters her ideals and goals on an almost daily

(and occasionally, several times a day)

basis.

(Harriet would definitely one day like to be a member of the literary elite[25]

---

[25] If Harriet ever gets to become a member of the literary elite, she hopes that she will get a chance to write about how nice Astoria is. That is where she lives now. She likes it. She likes that she can afford to live there and that the neighbors are very nice. She likes the lady at the laundromat who gave Harriet some laundry detergent when Harriet forgot hers at home and who refused to take any money for it, and the girl, or young woman, rather, who works at the laundromat and is almost always smiling and cheerful – two traits people tend not to associate with New Yorkers.

one day, but plugs along without health care and with a little bit of debt and with freedom in writing what she wishes to write.))

who was recently complaining about last minute changes in proofs and such and doesn't think that it really matters what page the advertising reference was made.))

when she was supposed to be changing trains, she was not paying attention

(She was listening to her iPod[26]

---

[26]Even when Harriet lived in San Francisco, soon after moving back to America from volunteering in Belize, when she was in one of her "capitalism-is-so-wrong" phases, she still loved the Apple Company, maybe because it was the first computer she got to use at school. She learned how to use Apple Logo and loved it. Even though the *Commodore 64* was still the greatest computer, if you can even call it that, ever. In any case, Harriet always had a soft spot for Apples. She did "conform" when she went to college and purchased a practical PC, but as soon as she was out on her own in the big, bad world of adulthood, she moved to a Mac. She loved the ad campaign in California about people switching from PCs to Macs. She even wanted to work for a Mac-based company. And, actually, now will be when she starts her new job on Monday.

(if she does get her job in advertising she would absolutely love to write an ad campaign for iPods)

(probably to R.E.M.,)

and almost missed her stop. She ran off the subway just in time, didn't realize that she had left one of her gloves. She was rearranging her bag on the bench right near the subway car when she saw

(out of the corner of her eye)

...

She loved the underdog, and so she loved Apple. And, she loves that iPods are doing so well, and only wishes she had bought some of their stock back when barely anyone owned an iPod – but she has very little money.

That is a lie – that is not Harriet's only wish....

She wants to do a series of thirty-second commercials wherein a cute, naïve-looking twenty-something-year-old man rides a crowded subway. People look angry. He has his music on his iPod and is smiling like an idiot. We take him to the MOMA on the really crowded, free night. While everyone is loud and pushing, he is staring at a Kandinsky painting while listening to R.E.M.'s "Walk Unafraid." The series goes on. He is walking and sees a girl listening to her iPod. She smiles at him. We then hear her music – completely different from his. That sort of thing.

iPods cut us off from the outside world, in a sense, but help us to stay in it, by helping us protect ourselves from audio irritants.

her black glove come whizzing by. It took a split second for her to realize that someone on the train had realized she had left her glove and was giving it back to her before the train went away.))

4. The security guard at One Penn Plaza was very nice to her.

(She was nervous about the interview for the job in advertising and the security guard unknowingly calmed her nerves.

(He pronounced her name the Polish[27, 28] way.

---

[27]Sometimes friends of Harriet get annoyed with her insistence on "being Polish." Harriet is a third generation American; in fact, she is a third-generation Massachusettsian, in fact, in fact, she is a third-generation Stoughtonian. However, Harriet likes being Polish as she thinks it gives her full permission to be stubborn and prideful. She used to have a running list of famous, smart Polish people:

- Pope John Paul II
- Copernicus
- Chopin
- Lech Walesa
- Martha Stewart

Harriet thinks the list must be longer than that, but is on her way on the Metro North train towards Riverdale on the Croton-Harmon Line and is distracted by the beauty of Harlem at 8:29 a.m. She is thinking about Langston Hughes and wants you to think about him as well. In fact, she would like you to go to your

Elizabeth Dembrowsky

>   (Harriet's last name is Zabrosky
>   but her most recent email address
>
>   (of many –
>
>   (over five))

---

bookshelf, bookstore, or library and get, buy, or borrow his collected poems and read some aloud in a room while listening to jazz music. Harriet recommends Charlie "Bird" Parker or John Coltrane, but is aware that she is not a jazz aficionado and realizes that you, idle reader, may indeed know a bit more about jazz than she does.

Harriet has a friend who thinks that something about Wally's should be inserted here.

Harriet wishes not to offend you with her apposition of "idle reader" but really likes that term and considers it one of endearment. Her boss wrote that in a poem he is working on that deals with death and love and fatherhood and the tsunami that killed thousands and thousands and thousands of people. By the way, idle reader, Harriet wishes to use a term of endearment because, if you have gotten this far, you have endeared yourself to Harriet. She is easily endeared, which might make you feel cheap and not-at-all special, however Harriet tends to tell people (a lot) that she finds them endearing. It will either annoy or charm you--or possibly both if you are one of those complicated-contradictory-intense types.

[28]At this particular edit of the book, Harriet recently received an e-mail from a colleague from graduate school who was visiting the United States and New York City on a grant. The friend e-mailed Harriet a copy of her grant report that she had to submit to her funders on return to the U.K. Harriet smiled to see the following lines included in the text of the e-mail:

> *Also, I am greatly indebted to my friend Harriet Zabrosky, an aspiring New York writer of Polish origin (I know the word Polish would make her happy), who taught me how to be a flâneuse in Manhattan, how to let my writerly enterprise become inspired by the morphing spirit of the street. I shall always remember the Sunday afternoons when we walked the Museum Mile on Fifth Avenue together between the Museum of the City of New York and the Met or the evening at the Bowery Poetry Club where some of the most radically activist writing in the city took shape and substance.*

lists her name as
Zabroskaya[29]

(which is the name the monk used when he created the account for her

Harriet is not sure if that is the Russian or the Polish version of her surname

(*Surname*[30] is British for last name. Just like *boot* is *truck* and *bonnet* is *hood*.)

---

[29]The monk was very nice to Harriet – sometimes. Sometimes he was not nice to Harriet, and sometimes he made her cry – and not just because she was in love with him and he was becoming a monk – sometimes he said things to her that really upset her – and asked her very personal questions that made her question all sorts of things that she didn't like to question.

He used to help her by forwarding emails to her when she lived in Devon, England, and her computer was acting strange. He started the new account for her so that she would be able to access her emails while she was in Devon.

One thing that the monk said that upset her is that she ought to be friends only with people that can help her in some way. She found that to be extremely un-Christian and remembered many of the reasons why she left organized religion – they could be summed up in the following word: hypocrisy.

> but it is the name she likes.)
>
> (Harriet's family in America spells its name wrong.
>
> > (which is very funny because of all those Polish jokes about Polish people being stupid
> >
> > > (which they aren't. Harriet

---

[30] By the way, if you ever want to get a British person mad, (although, I don't know why you would want to do that) refer to British as a language. If you were previously in doubt of the emotional depths of the British as a people and find them to be very emotionally withdrawn, if not barren,

(by the way,

• Alexandra Johnson – you don't count in that – but you're really Irish anyway, so you didn't really count to begin with. And, yes I am fully aware that that comment is offensive. Alex, I hope, knows that I don't mean to offend her, I just mean to have that particular offensive comment there.

• Ms. Paige, please don't take offense; it was my first impression, and if you weren't as poised and gorgeously emotionally restrained as you are, I probably wouldn't love you as much as I do. Well, that's a lie. As long as you made that great bread, I would love you as much as I do.

• Rowena, you know that you are the most American of all Brits)

then this little exercise would prove you wrong.

thinks some of
the smartest
people are
Polish[31].))

They spell their name with a "y"
and not an "i."

It is considered the Russian way
by some people

(which is sort of funny,
because her Polish
grandmother didn't like
that her uncle found
out that they were really
also part Ukrainian – or
at least because the borders shifted so often – it
was never really definite
on whether they were
Polish or Russian or
Ukrainian)

(Though Harriet's
Uncle Jim

---

[31] And, don't tell Harriet's mother, but Harriet is secretly convinced that she is Jewish and the Ashkenazi Jews, Harriet argues, are the smartest of them all...

(who used to
look like
Superman
when he was
younger)

and Harriet's grandfather's
brother's family all use
the "i" and not the "y".)

(Harriet is not sure of
this, but she thinks
that when her family
"came over" they may
have passed through
Ellis Island, or some
one them did and
spelled their name
wrong then.

The joke in the family
was that they were too
dumb to know how to
spell their own name –
which isn't really a
funny joke considering
the trials and tribs these
first folks had here, but

> ehhh, sometimes third generationres get a bit ignorant about trials and tribs they don't go through.)))))

And he and Harriet talked about the future of Poland and the E.U. and things like that.)

He walked her to the elevator and everything.

(Harriet had to buy a new outfit for the interview, even though she didn't want to.

> (Harriet is not like the stereotypical American woman in that she does not like to shop for clothes.)

> (and bought herself
>
>> (using her credit card)
>
> a pinstriped pair of pants and suit jacket with a pink camisole and pink high-heeled shoes.
>
>> (Not the pointy-shoes, though.)
>
>> (Harriet hates the pointy-shoes

(and the furry boots)

and thinks they make women look like witches.)))

5. The Muslim woman who helps her husband, or at least was helping her husband on Friday late afternoon/early evening on September 16th, 2005, on the corner of the street the MOMA is on and maybe Broadway or maybe 6th Avenue or maybe 7th Avenue with his cart of falafel, and gyros, and pita, and "salad," and white sauce, and hot sauce, and tomatoes, and onions, and rice – yellow or brown, and lamb, and beef, and peppers, gave Harriet a falafel sandwich for three dollars because it was all Harriet had, even though the regular price was four dollars.

That might not seem so significant, but Ariel Sharon and George Dubya and the Pakistani leadership – and almost everybody who runs a country – or at least represents someone who runs a country, or at the very least themselves represent a country, were a few blocks away pontificating.

The Muslim lady and Harriet made eye contact, and Harriet thanked her, and she told me with her eyes, "It's okay. I know you would do it for me if the situation were reversed, and, even if not, we have to help each other out when we can. Life is tough enough as it is … for you and for me."

And Harriet answered her with her eyes, "Yes, you are right, the people in control don't have a clue to what really living life is, they don't know what it is to make gyros all day, or to work with silly databases full of information that doesn't really need to be put in a database. They don't know what it is to deal with ignorant customers who treat me as an alien or bosses who do the same. We know these things – and we also know that pontificating is for the owl from *Winnie the Pooh*, but really ought to only exist in a book about stuffed animals that walk and talk, eat huney, and get stuck in entrances to their friend Rabbit's house." And then Harriet blinked before adding, "So thanks again for the three dollar falafel sandwich – I bet it will be the tastiest one I have ever had."

And it was.

6. New Yorkers don't kill each other often, a surprising phenomenon considering the great number of people living here, their ranges of viewpoints, religions, sexual orientations, politics, philosophies and senses, or lack, of style.

10

She was also an "activist." She can laugh about that now, but she still believes in the same things. She remembers the energy she put into a lot of different directions, trying to change things.

(Things can still change. Harriet promised herself to always believe that. She never wants to laugh at young people

(or old people)

who try to change things. Harriet has great respect for them and wants to give them money when she is rich.

By the way, she will be rich. I am certain of it, as is Nneka Jenkins who was Harriet's best friend in the first grade when the two were in "advanced reading" in the first grade. As is Gloria, Harriet's best friend from college who is the character that the publisher wishes to see more of in these pages

(maybe this is a good time to tell the skeletal version of a story that made Harriet learn that there really is no such thing as unconditional love between humans. Harriet used to believe in unconditional love – in high school religion class the concept was taught to the young women as something of which only G-d was capable. That idea didn't sit well with Harriet. She was convinced that she was capable of it too – and she tried to practice it for many years.

She promised her unconditional love to her closest friends and though most rolled their eyes at her, a few believed it.

One day, when Gloria was living in Brighton, Massachusetts

> (which is really just a part of Boston),

the worst thing that had happened in her life happened. Harriet was living in Belize at the time. Harriet should have gotten on the first plane to Boston, but she didn't.

Love is an action – it is not an idea. Unconditional love requires getting on the first plane to Boston when someone to whom you have promised unconditional love has the worst thing possible happen in her life. It does not involve telephone calls and letters and even prayers – it requires a physical presence that involves an action and not an idea.

Love is not what a wide-eyed American girl thinks she feels for a Romanian poet-soon-to-be-a-monk. Love is an action in everyday and extraordinary-day life. Love is presence and does not involve telephone calls and letters and even prayers — though there are times when those are nice things — they are not Love — they may be sweet tokens, but they are not Love.

(Harriet was recently in Massachusetts,

(in fact she is in Massachusetts right this minute.)

she wanted to ask her father, who is in Florida right this minute, about the story that she only recently learned even existed:

The story of the sister who jumps off the train heading to Siberia

Harriet never even knew that there had been a sister. She knew about the train — in fact, she's written an awful poem comparing contemporary self-appointed *cognoscentis* of New York with people being sent to Siberia on trains. She did not know, however, that anyone, especially the sister, had jumped off that train.

(Just like she never learned that her great-grandmother fled Spain until she went to Balboa on Easter alone in the spring of 2004, less than three weeks after the Madrid bombings[32]

³²Leaving the Church alone on Easter for my mother

she was stronger, stronger than I ever knew
and stubborn and Spanish,
as I am as well, though I never knew,
though I never knew her, or the story of her
leaving the church
where dirty hands claimed holiness and touched her dancing legs
later beaten by a different father
who called her *puta* and other things
— I won't translate for you —
leaving the church
only for her daughter to marry back into it
    los ninos de su nina favorita —
    totas catholicas tambien:
the irony, Mother, the irony.
and for you to have me.
and for you to have me three removed from her
and for you to have- three removed from me —
from her leaving the church to me leaving the church —
three removed from her.

and, so alone on Easter,
scared of the scary man that followed me
down gorgeous streets
of closed shoppes
of higher fashion than
we can afford
to do more
than walk down
and by and away from
the scary man alone on Easter, I was there.
I was there, far from you and *mi hermana* in her new home, temporary,
like mine always are; both drifting on different shores
as turtles-
    she is a steady-tortoise, I a moody-snapper,
we have learned to pack light but bring pencils, plenty of erasers,
    and lots and lots of stamps.
I learned then from you having just gone to a church and taken
for the first time in many lives of mine —
something that she probably spit out in anger.
I felt the same, Mother
scared of a Man, alone on Easter
a man alone on Easter —
scared of a man, alone on Easter.

she was stronger, stronger than I ever knew
and stubborn and Spanish
as am I, as are you.

because she was abused by a priest and her father did not believe her. And that her father beat her and she still refused to go to church and instead married the first man who would help her escape and he did – taking her all the way to Quincy, Massachusetts, where she joined the first Christian but NOT Catholic church she could find and worked as a seamstress at home while her husband wandered the streets claiming to look for but not really looking very hard for work and went to the black-and-white movies a lot – Buster Keaton was her favorite.)

The jumping off the train interested Harriet, a lot. Did the sister know how bad things were going to get, or did she want an excuse to get out of this whole life deal anyway and thought Siberia and the strong lack of desire to go there would be a good excuse to get out early of this whole life deal anyway? Harriet asked her dad who had never heard the story before his wife, Harriet's mother, mentioned it. Harriet found this odd as it was Harriet's father and not Harriet's mother who had the relatives who had gone to Siberia. Harriet's father suggested she call Walter – one of the brothers who had indeed been to Siberia and, though he is old, would most likely remember whether or not there was a sister and whether or not she jumped off the train.

Harriet's mother told her to walk to visit him at the house near the church. She told Harriet that he usually spent the "mornings with Adele at the cemetery." Adele is dead.

Harriet thought about this man, her grandmother's cousin, for a few minutes and decided that she did not need to ask him about the sister – that maybe it is not so important. That regardless of whether this particular sister existed and regardless of whether or not she did or did not jump from the train, that there must have been other sisters of other families that did that – and the sentiment is a tragic one – and that there is not a need to find out from Walter who spends a large part of his day, Harriet thinks, thinking about sad things, about this sad thing that Harriet thinks she has a right to know about.

Love is also visiting the cemetery everyday to be with your wife who has died. Love does not have to be that, but that action is most definitely love. Especially if you talk to your wife and not necessarily out loud.

Talking to someone who has died usually makes one cry, but that is okay – Love can be tears and that is not necessarily a bad thing.)

By the way – Love also means definitely having to say you're sorry – and it also means definitely meaning it when you say it.))

11

Christopher Klaskin just said yesterday that he thinks Harriet will be rich. Cara Maltz believes it, as does Rose Dias, and Sally Jane has made Harriet promise to let her live rent-free in her pool house after Harriet "strikes it rich." There are a gaggle of believers.)

One of the crimes that Harriet most opposed at this time

(and still does)

is murder. This may be why *Crime and Punishment* had such an impact on her.

(Other books of noteworthy influence on her include:

Catcher in the Rye
    (a given)
Pride and Prejudice
    (another given)
On the Road
1984

(but not *Animal Farm* – though Harriet's friend would argue, "C'mon! it's great, 'All animals are equal but some animals are more equal than others.'" Harriet's friend would argue that if this was her book – but it isn't. This is the same friend way back when who wanted something about Wally's inserted here. Maybe this friend should write her own book – rumor is, she is – but that it's about Anastasia the "lost" Russian princess or some such story.)

The Unbearable Lightness of Being
Miss Rumphius
Mao II
All I Need To Know I Learned in Kindergarten
The Hitchhiker's Guide to the Galaxy
Cat's Cradle
Still Life with Woodpecker
The Third Chimpanzee
The Selfish Gene
Tao Te Ching
The Awakening
The Autobiography of Malcolm X
The Bridge Across Forever
Are You There God? It's Me, Margaret
Harriet the Spy

(It has been a while since a book has made an impact on Harriet. There are books that she has read that were very well written and that she almost considers works of art (including, but not limited to:

Disgrace
Youth
    (both by JM Coetzee)
Enduring Love
Comfort of Strangers
    but not *Saturday*
    (all by Ian McEwan)
The History of Love
    (by Nicole Krauss)
A Heartbreaking Work of Staggering Genius
    (ha ha! I've beat the critics to the punch.[33]
    AHWSG yes, Harriet has read it. She loved it.
    The British kids she talked to didn't like it.
    She thinks it is because they don't get it.
    Harriet thinks Eggers is grand

        (though she always refers to him as
        Edgars – and gets corrected by people).

Too bad he's married.

    (and a writer.)

    (Harriet doesn't want to date a writer –

---

[33] Speaking of beating the critics to the punch, *Brief Wondrous Life of Oscar Mao*. Yes, yes, yes. He beat us to the punch, but he was nice enough not to take all the sherbert and there is still some left for us; we are grateful. *Gracias*.

It would be too much _____
I don't know what, but too much something or other, and she just doesn't want to.

(I know, that is closed-minded of her, but she is closed-minded.)))

The Gospel According to Jesus Christ
Blindness
  (all by Jose Saramago)
The Issa Valley
  (by the Polish Nobel Prize Winner Czeslaw Milosz)
Lolita
  (by Nabokov)
The Short Fiction of Roald Dahl
The Short Fiction of Patricia Highsmith))

Harriet wrote the following

(and if you find that her writing style and my narrative tone are in any way close to one another, please understand that it both is and is not a coincidence. Harriet is not me. I am not Harriet. This is not an autobiography. This is not a memoir – the market is glutted with that navel-gazing rubbish.)

I was worried that when I studied writing, I would be ruined to the fun of literature. I don't necessarily think that I am, but maybe now I read books for their style and experiments and for the craft than for its potential effect on me. I hope that I still can allow a book to impact me.

(The monk wants that book to be the Bible.*)*

(I went to Catholic school for six years where we had to read the Bible

(though not cover to cover),

and my favorite part was the New Testament. As much as I like   Judaism

(which is a lot)

I always found the Yahweh of the Moses era to be such a grumpy, old man.

(Yes, I am aware that religion is not meant to be a pick and choose type thing; however, as I tend to believe all religions are man-made, and that religion can help people to be better people

(in the sense that they treat themselves, other people, and the earth in nicer ways),

I do wish to practice some form of religion.

It tends to take a lot of things from a lot of different places.

Ultimately, however, it comes down to what I like to call

THE JESUS PRINCIPLE.

You know, the

Do unto others as you would have done unto you.[34]

I like that. A lot.[35]

Especially because I think it means a lot of different things at the same time.

Take for example, my friend Gloria

(the molecular biologist or geneticist or what-have-you-ist),

who is very self-reliant and lives alone in NYC

supports herself, and almost never needs to ask for directions.

---

[34]Harriet doesn't know that the Jesus Principle was around long before Jesus; essentially, Christ was plagiarizing, but most have justly allowed for that, considering all the other fabulous things associated with this extraordinary life.

[35]Actually, Harriet is liking Judaism more and more as she is currently working for the United Jewish Communities. When she isn't busy making adjustments to Excel, Word, and Access documents, or sending pithy emails to friends, or editing Gloria's essays for business school, or making trips to get more coffee—which, by the way, is not nearly as good as the stuff at the Local Initiative for Something Beginning with an S- Corporation, or writing out a marketing plan and a mission statement for her new venture as a t-shirt designer/seller, she reads the *Orchard*, a 35-page, densely-written, but well-designed pamphlet/magazine/thingy about the holiday season that is approaching. In fact, Harriet will have NINE unpaid days off next month as the organization closes for a series of holidays. She reads the *Orchard* and takes notes on things like *korban* which means "expression of intimate relationship understood as traveling" or *tzadik* which means "righteous soul trapped in one of the broken shards."

> *For her--the* Do unto others *part is very simple. It translates into, "Leave me alone and I'll leave you alone."*
>
> *(Don't get me wrong--she isn't some callous, heartless person*
>
> *(not in the least).*
>
> *(It's just that she doesn't need help from people all that much.)*
>
> *She would prefer space from people and gives people space.*
>
> *For me, the principle is different. It means lots of gifts and cards and hugs and surprises and nice dinners and long letters.*
>
> *This is a lot of work, but I want all those things for me, so I have to do it.*
>
> *(In case you are wondering, this has paid off in different ways.*[36]

---

[36] 1. On my nineteenth birthday, my friends from high school and college got together and bought me a car. It wasn't a really nice one – in fact, it died within the week, and it cost me more to have the car towed than my friends paid for the car itself. The thing is, they researched and found a car just like the one that I had driven for three years and that had recently died (a Ford Fairmont station-wagon), bought it, and drove it to Boston to surprise me.

2. On my 21st birthday, I was studying archaeology in Belize and had only been there for a few weeks. I was sad to not have my friends nearby to celebrate being legally allowed to drink. But my best friend from home (the one that is married--remember...the banana dress and everything) bought a cake that said, "Happy 21st Harriet" and took an entire roll of photos of people from her work and my college friends and my neighbors in Boston

holding the cake. The final pictures were of my friends smoking the brand of cigarettes I used to smoke and toasting me. Actually, the final photos were of them shmooshing cake in each other's faces. The second to last photo was of my friends smoking the brand of cigarettes I used to smoke and toasting me.

3. Before I went to live in Belize for the first time, my friends threw me a grand party wherein they presented me with a box full of letters from everyone at the party and from some people who couldn't make it to the party – that all included funny things about what they would miss about me when I was gone and advice as to what to do in the jungle and other just nice, sweet things.

4. My friends in America had planned a "Welcome Home, Harriet" party for me, but I missed it. They held the party anyway and made a home-movie about it, making fun of me and sending me special messages.

5. A homeless man that I knew in Boston gave me a t-shirt. (I knew a lot of homeless men in Boston, and in Cambridge, because I made a film about homelessness for part of my senior thesis in college. The film is called Street Stories and even though it is definitely "student-film quality" it makes the point that it was supposed to make; there are a few copies of it hanging around somewhere–you could probably find it if you looked in the right places.)

6. On my 24th birthday, when I was living in San Francisco, my roommates gave me a great present. They bought a plane ticket for my best friend from home (who didn't have very much money at the time–and never really got to go anywhere to visit) to visit me. I cried.

7. When I held a launch for the anthology that I served as editor and publisher for in the U.K., my writers gave me a gorgeous necklace (that I wear often and think of them). I think it is very funny that they gave their publisher a gift–it is usually the publisher that gives the writers the gifts (but I think they know how hard I worked on it.) One of the nicest things about the necklace is that it "matches" a bracelet that one of my best friends from college brought back from Croatia for me. When I wear them together, not only do I look "well-accessorized" or whatever the term is for someone whose jewelry is coordinated, but I also feel as if I am carrying with me the spirit of both my undergrad and graduate school college friends. I smile a lot when I am "well-accessorized."

8. Before I moved to NYC, my friends in Boston and Cambridge and the area threw me a White Trash Intellectuals Going-Away Party. (When I was in England, I started a company called White Trash Intellectuals – well, really I started a bank account – which I

Not always, though – part of the reason,

(I tend to think)

I am so poor

(financially).)

---

essentially had to empty when I was last in England to pay for my trip to England and my expenses while there). My friend Erica (the gregarious one that lived in NYC right after college) even made tater tots. The guests all wrote poems, too, some of them silly – well, all of them silly, but all of them sort of nice and sweet as well.

9. On my 27th birthday, it was my fourth day of living in NYC, my roommate surprised me with a container of Dunkin Donuts Coffee Beans, and I didn't even know that she knew it was my birthday.

12

Many people,

    (and this includes Harriet)

like to see themselves as moral and upright citizens of the world, or at the very least moral and upright citizens of their country.

Reading a book, or seeing a play or a dance performance, or watching a film that questions the self-image of being moral and upright citizens of the world, or at the very least moral and upright citizens of their country, can often be very disturbing.

Crime and Punishment did that for Harriet – it scared her; she felt as if she were capable of killing someone.

    (However, this does not mean that if Harriet did go and kill someone that it would be the fault of

    Fyodor – or
    The publisher, or

The Russian people,
The book clerk, or
The friend that recommended the book.

> (**Explain, not Excuse.** That's Harriet's view on psychology and exploring the reasons why people do what they do.))

These are scary thoughts to have. Harriet later read *Notes from the Underground* and a similar thing happened.

> (She bought the Dover edition and underlined many lines and phrases that struck her as interesting or true.

>> (Harriet does that to a lot of books.

>>> (On rare occasion, she does this to ones that she takes out of the library.

>>>> (One of Harriet's other favorite aunts is a librarian and would be sorry to learn that Harriet ever defaced a library book.

>>>>> (Though, Harriet would love to see one of her books defaced by a reader from the library – because it would prove that it had been read.)))))

The reason why she associated Dostoyevsky with the monk is actually a bit complicated:

- The monk, at least before he became a monk and had to grow a beard and wear a black cloak everyday, had a very intense face.

  (Harriet's mother, who later described the monk

  (after looking at a picture of him)

  as having a face "you could write a book about."

- He was very skinny and tall and had dark hair and dark eyes.

  (Actually, Harriet isn't so sure that his eyes were dark –

  (One should really remember the color of the eyes of someone you fall in love with, but Harriet avoided looking into the eyes of the monk, because she knew she would cry if she did.))

- When he spoke, he did so in a tone

(of such great confidence)

(bordering on arrogance)

that Harriet was not very accustomed to.

He was very sure of himself and extremely opinionated.[37]

- He seemed very Eastern European and almost Russian, as if he:

    - had come right out of the eighteen hundreds, or
    - had been alive during the Bolshevik Revolution, or
    - was a character in a Chekhov story, or
    - was the spoiled son of an oligarch who was
      cut off from the cash flow because
      he wanted to be a "poet."

---

[37]In fact, there is a great story of the first day of the active writing workshop, where Harriet had brought her work to be analyzed; the monk said in his fantastic accent, "If I didn't have to read this for class, I would have put it down after the first page." After a year of workshops, one does become used to that sort of criticism and really actually can tend to enjoy it, but for a wide-eyed, idealistic American girl those were harsh words from the cute, skinny boy with the nice accent.

He later told her that it was actually the best novel start he had read out of all the writers in the class.

She wrote about this in the currently unpublished but very available *Daffodils and Bad Coffee*. It could be compared to Bill Bryson.

- He wrote very strange fiction. The tutor in the class

    (this is British for professor – although the duties are a bit different from an American concept of professor)

    had said that the monk's writing reminded him of Dostoyevsky and the monk was highly pleased and responded that he considered the man to be a genius[38]

---

[38]The monk never even read *Brothers Karamazov* – which Harriet found ironic.

She had written to him about reading the book, and he responded that he had tried when he was younger but that he could never get through it. There are many people that claim *Brothers Karamazov* as their favorite book – having never read it.

By the way, rumor has it Marilyn Monroe's favorite book was *Brothers Karamazov*. Rumor also has it that she wanted to play the part of Grushenka in the Hollywood version of *Brothers Karamazov*, but was not given the part. Rumor also has it that Arthur Miller wrote the screenplay *The Misfits* for her as a "Sorry you didn't get the part of Grushenka in the Hollywood version of *Brothers Karamazov*, but here is a very interesting role that I wrote for you and is a character that in many ways resembles the way that I view you" gift. It was the last movie that Marilyn was in. It was also the last movie that Clark Gable or Rock Hudson or one of those guys, the one who plays her love interest in the movie, ever did as well.

The Brooklyn Museum of Art had a showing of photographs of Marilyn Monroe up during the Spring of 2005 also running at the same time as a show of the work of Basquiat. Basquiat is rumored to have dated Madonna. It is also rumored that Jackie O refused to meet Madonna when her son was dating Madonna. Marilyn Monroe is rumored to have had an affair with Jackie O's first husband. It is also rumored that Jackie O's first husband and brother-in-law were involved with the premature death of Miss Marilyn Monroe. Marilyn's first name was actually Norma Jean. Madonna's first name is actually Madonna.

- The monk was a Christian Orthodox, as was Dostoyevsky. Both men

  (it seems strange to describe the monk as a man — he is more of a boy, even though he would like to have thought of himself as a man).

  wrote with the hopes of making people understand the need to be Orthodox Christian. The monk wrote poetry and Dostoyevsky wrote novels.

- The monk liked to be compared to Dostoyevsky and had even asked Harriet to do so in a poem.

  (which she didn't.

  (she had written a poem called "Baroque" that starts like this—   A rough pearl:
  A clumsy grace
  All heart and turmoil
  Tolstoy and Christie on a rope swing
  Debating the merits of following form

)

In any case, there are other books that people also like for people to think they have read, even when they haven't. Some of these books include:

G-d's *The Bible*
Thomas Pynchon's *Gravity's Rainbow*
David Foster Wallace's *Infinite Jest*
Stephen Hawking's *Brief History of Time*
Elizabeth Dembrowsky's *My Monk*

Just checking to see how close a reader you are....

She had instead referred to the monk as Tolstoy – as in Leo Tolstoy. She did this for a few reasons:

1. The monk's real name

>(before becoming a monk and changing it to Seraphim)

>(and not his pseudonym – Adrian Urmanov)

>is/was Leonard. Harriet called him Leo, and sometimes Harriet called him Leon. And later, when Harriet would talk about him to friends back in America, she would refer to him as "My Monk"

>(Ding! Ding! Ding!

>>(said loudly and quickly and sharply)

>The title of the book. Yes. You've got it, now back to the list…)

2. Tolstoy fits the rhythm of the poem better.

>(by the way, Christie is after Agatha Christie, the crime-fiction writer from Devon. That name represents dear, sweet, lovely, British Deborah who Harriet adores and misses. British Deborah is everything that is good and Middle Class about England. British Deborah-Sweet-Deborah speaks with a superb, unaffected BBC accent .)

3. She had recently been reading Chekhov, including a short story called "The Black Monk." She didn't think that her Leo was at all a "black monk" in any creepy sense, but she had really enjoyed the story ... and Chekhov was on her mind and so was Tolstoy.))

13

In any case, the monk had gone to Russia after leaving the U.K. and Harriet had gone to Germany.

(She has a very good friend

(named Sarah-Lee)

who was born in Hamburg.

(This very good friend's father is American and a journalist who taught himself German when he moved to Hamburg instead of to Vietnam in the time when a lot of American men were moving to Vietnam, some of them temporarily, and some of them forever, and her mother is German and a nurse who does not speak English fluently. However, it often appears that, in a sense, rather than being a girl with two countries, sometimes she tends to be a girl with no country

(: her German friends tend to think of her as American, and her American friends tend to think of her as German).

(When she was growing up in Germany, she used to take trips to Disney World when she was young and her dad used to make her listen to lots of rock music and watch all the great classic American movies.)

(And, in America,

(specifically in Massachusetts, where she lives

(she lived on Martha's Vineyard and in Boston and now lives in Cambridge, on the border of Somerville[39,40]))

---

[39]Actually, she is soon moving back to Hamburg, and possibly after that to Kracov or Warsaw, which makes Harriet very jealous because Harriet does not have E.U. citizenship and for Harriet to move to either of those two cities, which Harriet would love to do, would be much more difficult).

In any case, Harriet wishes Sarah-Lee well and hopes that this move is a good one for her.

[40]In fact, Sarah-Lee, who some of Harriet's friends used to refer to as either "German Sarah" or "Sarah the German," now lives back in Hamburg and forgot to pay a phone bill, actually a couple of phone bills, for the cell phone that Harriet had given to her when Harriet moved to England. Harriet found this out one very sad day when she tried to apply for a re-mortgage loan on a lil, adorable and decrepit shack in New Hampshire and her friend Vincent Bettes who is a loan processor for the First Republic Bank wrote her an email something along the lines of:

Brosky, Just wanted you to know – a Sprint phone bill from 2003 was sent to a collection agency because it was never paid. Thought you might want to know.
–Vin

sometimes when she says things, she comes across as being severe and strict – a trait people tend to associate with Germans.

This is sort of funny, because Sarah-Lee is very, very kind and gentle and very, very sensitive

(and also not a very good house keeper)

and is not a severe person at all.

However, most of us are not the people we sometimes come across as being.))

This friend invited her to spend a month in Hamburg after Harriet had finished up her studies in the U.K. Harriet had one final deadline in August, but knew that she wanted to enjoy her time in Germany fully and so she got her work done ahead of time.

(Harriet can be a huge procrastinator

(like most of us)

but sometimes can really focus and get things done ahead of time,

(like most of us)

and this was one of those occasions.)

Harriet was thrilled. She had just started rewriting her novel-in-progress as a screenplay[41] and was excited about having time to both write and relax.

And Harriet felt very sophisticated about the fact that she was spending a month in Germany writing. She felt as if she were living her dream.

(Harriet loved reading about

- Anais Nin,
- Henry Miller,
- Gertrude Stein,
- Ernest Hemingway,
- Allen Ginsberg
- and even Johnny Depp –

who all left America for a while to work on their craft in Europe

(although Harriet isn't sure that Johnny Depp is working on his craft

(unless his craft involves speaking in a "European tone of voice" and criticizing U.S. culture

(Madonna does this a bit, too.)

---

[41]This is the same screenplay that Harriet's agent would later find to be too "intellectual."

(Harriet does it, too, even though she has no money and no fame – she still follows the trend of criticizing her homeland[42]

---

[42]Samuel Clemens, a.k.a. Mark Twain, is remembered as saying, "Loyalty to the country always. Loyalty to the government when it deserves it." He also said something along the lines of, "If at the end of your life, you can count your friends on one hand, you are a lucky man."

Harriet never agreed with that second statement when she first learned it in high school, as she was quite the social butterfly back then, but she has since really come to appreciate what she thinks Mr. Clemens meant when he said/wrote that.

He also said, or at least Harriet thinks that he also said, "A good book should be read three times in one's life: in boyhood, adulthood, and old age."

Yes, Harriet gives Mr. Clemens the same "get out of jail free card" that she offers Arthur Burgess when it comes to use of gender specific terms. Harriet finds it silly for people to argue with contemporary ideas about political correctness against people that can neither defend nor argue about their words.

Harriet loves that quote and thinks *Catcher in the Rye* means something different for her each time that she reads it.

Her friend, Chris-the-Aspiring-Politician, is only just now reading that book. Harriet is astonished that she never learned this before as they have been friends for over ten years, and she usually demands that people read that book. Or at least she used to demand; nowadays as a writer, she is much less demanding – except to her mother and her little sister – from whom she can't seem to not demand things (have no fear; Harriet is not remotely spoiled – no one listens to her demands, especially not her mother or her little sister.)

And she tries very hard not to be rude to people. She wishes that more people would try hard not to be rude to people. As she has traveled further down this path of writerdom- she has become more and more sensitive and inwardly judgmental and oddly critical and oddly sentimental.

Back to Mr. Clemens/Twain…

Recently, Harriet has been reading some of Sam's short fiction,

(Harriet does that even when she is in her homeland.

(Harriet wishes more Americans

- as well as some of the experimental plays of Federico García Lorca – Spanish, dead, one of his country's most widely regarded poets/dramatists,

- as well as the novels of Jose Saramago – Portuguese, dead, Nobel Prize Winner,

- and *Palace of Dreams* by Ismael Kadare – Albanian, alive (as of 5:37pm EST on the 7th of September 2005), Man Booker International Prize Winner,

- *Cloud Atlas* by David Mitchell, British-but-living-in-Ireland, cool-structure writer,

- *The Wind-Up Bird Chronicles* by Haruki Murakami, "Japan's most highly regarded novelist" according to his book jacket, and Harriet is enjoying the book, though her friend, Mara with the baby named Lyra, wrote as an inscription on the book

Harriet–
If someone were to ask me to explain
this book, I'd have no choice but to
to give them a vapid stare but I
know I felt a major sense of
Accomplishment upon completion.
            Love, Mara,

- *Kill Two Birds and Get Stoned* by Kinky Friedman – self-proclaimed "Texas Jewboy" who is running for Governor of Texas.)

Now back to Mr. T…

(as in Twain and not B.A. Baracas)

and is reminded of how smart and cynical Mr. C was. She gave a book of his short fiction to Lyra, the baby of her friends Mara and Dave and has read the baby a few of the stories. Lyra seems to enjoy the stories, or at least enjoys the silly faces and voices that Harriet uses when she is reading Lyra the stories.

> would criticize their homeland instead of going online to price shop for S.U.V.' s or whatever it is that Americans who do not criticize their homeland do with their spare time.))))))

Harriet felt very lucky to be able to have these experiences. Harriet always wanted these experiences, but somehow thought she would end up as a lawyer or a politician

   (perhaps – even working for the Foreign Service)

and not be working on a writing project in Hamburg when she was 26 years old.)

(Harriet had many dreams. Some of them have already come to pass. Others probably never will.)

14

During her entire month in Germany, she emailed the monk only once, to tell him that her grandmother's cousin in Poland had died and that she was going to drive there to go to the funeral. She was asking him to pray for her grandmother's cousin, a kind man who had been taken by the Russians at the beginning of World War II

(a lot of people in America don't know about what the Russians did during WWII.

They did things like come into Polish villages to round up all the people they considered to be intellectuals, or *intelligentsia*, and take them away.

Some of these people

(like John, the brother of the man who died in Poland in 2004

(and who very well might have been part of the Polish Resistance movement – though no one knows for sure).)

were never seen by their families again.

The Russians also took people and sent them to Siberia.

> (they took Eddie, the man who died in Poland in 2004, and his brother, Walter, who is still alive and lives in Stoughton, Massachusetts, and their mother, who died a long time ago.
>
>> (*note bene*: A not so idle reader may be experiencing something akin to *deja vu* here.)

Eddie, the man who died in Poland in 2004, ended up fighting on the side of the Allies for the British and lost his eye in battle

> (and had it replaced with a glass one that used to make Harriet nervous when she was a little girl and had to talk to him, because it always seemed as if he was looking somewhere else
>
>> (for people who live through a war "looking somewhere else" is something that they often do a lot.
>>
>>> (but in this particular instance, he was not doing that kind of "looking somewhere else;" he simply had a glass eye that wasn't looking anywhere in particular because it was glass and didn't work.)))

and came

(or went depending on your perspective)

to America after the war, where he worked in a factory until he retired, and was able to move back to Poland and be relatively rich and enjoy his final years back in a peaceful Poland.

(Harriet visited him twice in Lomza, Poland

(which is near the city of Bialystock

(which is near the city of Warsaw

(where Harriet and her little sister met a cute, Polish musician who was performing in a jazz bar.[43] He told the two sisters that the "Nazis destroyed the soul of the city."

(Harriet had, seconds before this comment of his, complimented him on the beauty of the rebuilt city of Warsaw))))

---

[43]Harriet wrote a short story that takes place in Poland for her submission for a module (British for "class") in graduate school that she called "The Life You Save May Be Your Own," also a title for a short story by Flannery O'Connor.

and learned about how nice his life was in this small town with his nice, Polish wife.

(Harriet absolutely adored his Polish wife, Boshena, who spoke very little English

(and who tried

(unsuccessfully)

to convince Harriet to learn Polish)

but somehow was able to communicate with Harriet and was a very sweet woman, who ate strawberries and smoked Russian black market cigarettes[44] and taught

---

[44]Harriet wrote about this in the poem "Baroque."

Baroque

Don't tell them
all strawberries will always be Polish
always
& forever
served with Russian black market cigarettes
eaten unwashed & swallowed whole without clotted-cream
without sugar & spice & everything nice

You cannot go back
to a place you have never been

You can try

You can try to
drive on into the east

Harriet a very important lesson.

At the time of her first visit to Poland, Harriet hated a lot of things about America,

like

- the School of the Americas

    (which is a military training base for Latin American military personnel based in Fort Benning, Georgia, and has since changed its name

    (or rather, had its name changed)

    to something more difficult to remember),

- or the trade embargo on Cuba

Harriet lied in the poem – sort of. She wrote "You cannot go back/ to a place you have never been." The lie is that she did go back – three times. So it was a place she had been. She was referring to Poland. However, she could not go back to the Poland that was there when her great-grandmother was. Which may be one of the reasons that she was so intrigued by the monk – he reminded her of a place that no longer existed. Even his Orthodoxy hadn't changed in two thousand years.

(Harriet had liked certain things about Fidel Castro

    (not his censorship of the press, or his arrest of political opponents, or his dictatorship and "I'm always right" attitudes)

like his initial idealism in wanting to make Cuba a better and more fair place.

    (Harriet wants to one day write a screenplay about Fidel Castro's honeymoon with his first wife that tells of when they came to New York City.

        (By the way, in case you were wondering, **New York City IS the best city in the world.** However, it is not the only city in the world. And we

            (and, yes, I put myself in that category)

    often forget that.)

        (She thinks it would be interesting to explore

Elizabeth Dembrowsky

what Fidel Castro was like before he became a revolutionary and then a communist and then a dictator.

(Remember --
Harriet is
*Intentionally
Naïve* --

(it
drives
her
brother
crazy
and her
uncle,
too,
because
they
think
she
could
have
been
an
engi-

neer or a politician had she not been so silly and *Intentionally Naïve* about things like wanting to know what sort of movies Fidel Castro went to see when he was in NYC))

Harriet liked the film *El Comandante* Stone made about Fidel Castro[45]))),

- or the practice of the death penalty

(that we have previously mentioned),

- or the refusal of either the American public or the American government to seriously examine its use of oil and how it can alter its priorities and means of commerce, travel, and recreation to involve a lessening of a dependence on oil, especially "foreign oil,"

---

[45]Harriet saw this movie while in the U.K. She saw it on the recommendation of a very cute Masters in Finance student from Mexico who talked to her on the double-decker bus ride from the campus to the place she was living, on Beehive Road in Kenilworth, Warwickshire. The boy, Harriet thought, was trying to flirt with her on the bus and told her to see the movie on Monday night. Harriet was a bit hesitant, because she was still in love with the monk, and even though she knew it was silly because he was going to be a monk, she was a little scared about going on dates with very cute Masters in Finance students from Mexico. If you know the movie *Yentl* very very well, you might know that there is a Talmudic reference there that relates to this. The funny thing is, she did go to see the film and looked for the very cute Masters in Finance student, but didn't see him...until later when she was waiting for the bus, and she saw him kissing a very pretty Latin American girl at the bus stop. Harriet was embarrassed and a little bit angry, but she smiled at him anyway and got on the bus and sat very far away from him.

She also had a crush on her Spanish roommate--but it was a completely harmless one. He had a girlfriend in Spain and was only going to be in England temporarily, sort of like Harriet. However, the two were very good friends, and the Spanish roommate, who was a veterinarian specializing in cardiology, used to make great

- or the "Two-Party System" that seems to dominate mainstream politics,

- or the increases in the national debt,

- or the decrease in financial support for The Arts,

- or many, many other things that will not be mentioned

   (remember, this is not a political book)

here and now

   (or there and later, either

      (wherever there and later is)))

Harriet blamed Hollywood and the culture of the cult of celebrity for distracting people from knowing and caring about what their country was doing to other countries on the globe.

(there is a line from an Ani DiFranco song

---

food for Harriet, and he would take her to see movies and would pay her to help him with edits on his papers about heart abnormalities of dogs and cats and with general conversational English. Sometimes, they would even watch television together, which means a lot, because Harriet absolutely hates television.

(Harriet really, really enjoys the music of Ani DiFranco

(although not as much now as she did when she was in her late teens and early twenties).

and considers her to be a very "Righteous Babe," as her record label name suggests.

("Her" in the previous sentence refers to one Ms. Ani DiFranco and not to one Ms. Harriet Zabrosky. Ms. Harriet Zabrosky does not, yet, have a record label

(though, she does have a publishing company, called White Trash Intellectuals)).

(Harriet also likes the music of:

Leonard Cohen
Pixacota Five
R.E.M.
Nina Simone
Moby
Coldplay
Frank Sinatra,
Lakis Pavlou,[46] and
Sade.))

"putting America to sleep with warm milk and T.V.[47] "

---

[46]Lakis Pavlou is actually a friend of Harriet's. They met one night, back when his name was still Kevin, at the International House of Pancakes in Kenmore Square – remember back in the early pages the mention of this IHOP. Anyway, he was the busboy and she was a customer and he played "I Like American Music" on the guitar for her and her friends. Later, when he moved to New York and changed his name to Lakis – he ended up becoming friends with the lead singer of the Violent Femmes (the band who wrote "I Like American Music"). In fact, this past Thursday night, Lakis performed at the Satellite Bar on 6th Street between Avenues A & B. Harriet was there. The lead singer of the band Violent Femmes came and played the fiddle for two of Lakis' sets. It was pretty cool. Some sort of weirdly-shaped full circle.

[47]Harriet also likes the following lines from Ani DiFranco lyrics:

> I could make you happy, if you weren't already

> when I look down, I miss all the good stuff
> when I look up, I just trip over things

15

Harriet used to be a very big pain to her friends when she was in college because she was always ranting against U.S. Foreign Policy and unfair domestic practices and then protesting about it, without really having a clue as to how to fix things.)

that Harriet really liked.

(in fact, Harriet liked it so much that she quoted it in one of her essays for her Masters in Writing. She included both Ani DiFranco and Madonna lyrics.

(She used a line from Madonna's Song *American Dream*:

"I live the American dream
And I just realized that nothing is what it seems).")

Harriet was very sad when her grader accused her of having a "shrill" tone in her essay, when she wrote about the use of satire in American literary history and why in a Post 9-11 World, the use of satire can be dangerous.

> (Harriet wrote that her generation of Americans is so accustomed to satire that it no longer tends to spur change, or inspire individuals to improve a situation – rather, it simply reaffirms the feeling of:
>
> • helplessness and
> • futility in action and
> • a general malaise
>
>> (which is essentially the same thing as a feeling of futility in action, which is essentially the same things as a feeling of helplessness.).))

She

> (at this time in her life)

was very closed-minded because she shut her mind off to "all things Hollywood," in that she meant movies, television, and pop music.

But Boshena taught her an important lesson.

One night while staying in Poland at her cousin's house, she was having trouble sleeping. She got up and walked downstairs.

She was very embarrassed because she thought everyone was asleep, but Boshena was awake. She was crying.

Harriet didn't know what to do because her Polish was so limited. She knew that Boshena had had a very hard life and thought that maybe she was crying because she was remembering it.

But that was not why she was crying. She started to say to Harriet, "I am sorry. I am sorry. I am crying. I am sorry. The movie, the movie, oh so sad."

Harriet was confused, until Boshena pointed to the television.

There had been one in the room Harriet was sleeping in as well.

In fact, she had just watched the end of *Hero* with Dustin Hoffman and Julia Roberts, a movie that always made her cry,

    (even though it was blatantly sentimental and very scripted)

and she thought maybe it could make her sleepy

    (it didn't).

She realized that Boshena had been watching the same movie.

Then Boshena put the kettle on for tea and took out her Polish-English dictionary and started to tell Harriet about Jack Lemmon and how much she loved his movies.

Harriet still criticizes U.S. Foreign Policy and the culture of the cult of celebrity, but now she likes to watch movies and makes it a point to not feel bad about them[48]

>(Most people don't need to go all the way to eastern Poland to realize that movies can be soothing
>
>>(and can make us feel better sometimes by making us feel worse)
>
>and can be very inspiring as well. However, Harriet is not "most people.")

---

[48]Harriet was raised Catholic. She tends to feel bad about a lot of things. She went through her very anti-Catholic phase when she was in college, but she is over it. In fact, on occasion, she goes to church. She likes the idea of people getting together for a reason other than shopping, or yelling, or having things done for them. Being in a church full of people sometimes makes Harriet very happy. She sometimes thinks that maybe some of their belief will rub off onto her. Though sometimes she thinks they look at her and know that she is a faker. She appreciates that these people who might be looking at her and knowing that she is a faker don't say anything about it. She appreciates that at the part of the service where you are supposed to reach out and shake hands with the people in your pew, or the people in the pew either in front or in back of you, and say, "Peace" or "Peace be with you" that these people who might be looking at her and knowing that she is a faker still reach out to shake her hand.

The monk used to make her watch all sorts of movies[49] It was annoying, actually. She felt as if he was trying to educate her or something. She respected him as a poet, and even a critic of literature, but she really didn't want to sit through every movie that he thought was great. However, she did sometimes without complaining

(like when she really needed a break from writing and studying and working),

but other times she would get mad at him

(like when she was really tired and was staying at her friend British Deborah's flat and wanted to watch a light-hearted movie, or nothing at all, and the monk insisted that they watch *Who's Afraid of Virginia Woolf?*

(part of the reason why she got so mad at him was he kept saying that he always imagined his wife would be like the Elizabeth Taylor character

(though she didn't really get mad at him until later when her friend

(the German-American one)

told her that not only did Harriet look

---

[49]The monk made Harriet watch the following movies: *Evita, Dancer in the Dark, Policemen Wear Dresses, On Golden Pond, Who's Afraid of Virginia Woolf?*

> like Elizabeth Taylor
>
>> (or at least her eyes did)
>
>> but that the movie was an analogy of her relationship with the monk.))

and also that Harriet didn't understand what the movie was about.

Harriet didn't care what the movie was about. She cared that she was tired and didn't want to watch it, but that he insisted.

> (Harriet felt that the monk always insisted. She found him very spoiled
>
>> (but for some silly reason, she still loved to spend time with him).))).

16

Harriet's plans to be friends with Leo were not easily accomplished. True, from the start, he confided in her, but only in angry rantings about the university bureaucracy, the weather of England, and the idiocy of many of their coursework assignments. She listened to him patiently, hiding a smile at his seemingly endless negativity. Here he was, a full-scholarship recipient and there she was, paying her own way, having left the stability of family, work, and friends in the United States to learn the ridiculous task of "writing" in this so-very-foreign country, working on weekends, cleaning tables with workers so diverse that the United Nations might have fewer representatives in its chambers than she had working with her to serve overweight and demanding Brits baps with brown sauce and white coffees.

As the weeks went by, it turned out to be he rather than she that needed the time together, exclusively. It began with innocent sharing of candies – and soon morphed to include pilgrimages downstairs to the awful coffee machine – each taking turns to buy the other a disgusting cup that they would love and hate together. Their odd courtship was recognized by everyone except them. The Bosnian cleaning lady would cluck in approval when she saw them giggling together; the security guards would smile at closing time, allowing the couple as much time as they could to continue their "work" when all the other students had dutifully left hours before.

They both shared a need to live the writer's life, in whatever strange way they were creating it, he encouraging her to write more honestly - she hating his insistence on telling her what to do but trying to discover whatever it was that this elusive honesty could bring to her writing.

They began to refer to the computer lab as "home" and would even leave one another notes and presents there if they had to leave it for an extended period of time. She would complain to him about the overbearing landlord, and he would offer ridiculous attempts at help, "I will hang in a tree outside his house in a bag of water covered with poetry." That Oh so Romanian! form of performance art would do itself no good to a comptroller for the county of Warwickshire's expenditures – with a need to have each of his tenants itemize their share of the phone bill in an *Excel* spreadsheet. But Leo was somehow unintentionally worming his way into her thoughts before falling asleep – and would send her off with a smile on her face.

Love, Harriet wrote, *is a funny thing. I don't really understand it at all. I was a student of psychology and of anthropology when I first went to college and was interested in what love meant to individuals in different cultures throughout time.*

I was also interested in why people fall in love, and what genetic predisposition would make falling in love happen – and why, accepting Darwin's Theory of Survival of the Fittest, the particular trait of having the ability to fall in love survived throughout time.

Because it really doesn't have that much to do with sex. Or at least not in contemporary times.

But why do we "fall for" people who are not any "good for" us — for example, a man who is very critical and very impatient and very needy and demanding and was going to join a monastery?

Life really doesn't make sense; no matter how much you learn or how many books you read, or write.

17

Not only did he make her watch movies, but he also made her listen to music. Some of this music she really liked:

- Martin Gore
- Pet Shop Boys
- The complete R.E.M.
- Shirley Bassey
- Tina Turner
- Eric Satie[50]

(maybe)

---

[50] Eric Satie is/was a French composer who would write strange notes on his composition sheets. He would write things like "I want a hat of solid mahogany" and "from the ends of the eyes."

There was a children's book about Eric Satie in the music section of the Wellesley Booksmith, the independent bookstore where Harriet worked part-time before moving to NYC where she worked with her best friend Brenda who is the book receiver.

• and Leonard Cohen)

but some of the music was awful and that was the music that he didn't simply lend to her to listen to, but the

music he would insist on playing when the two of them were together in a place that had a CD player

(like Madonna's album
American Life
or George Michael))).

And the thing that was the most awful was that after he and she went in their opposite directions –

There are two people that she liked quite a bit from there – Erica who can be chaos on wheels but has a nice sense of humor and Barry who is also one of Harriet's favorite people that she has met since coming back from the U.K.

Harriet feels that books for children should be really books for children – and sneaky things like making your six-year-old into a member of the cultural elite is not why children's books were invented.

They were invented, she believes, to promote silliness and imagination, but she did enjoy reading the children's book about Eric Satie. In fact, she went to her local library (where they know her very well) and took out a CD that included his music. Harriet thought she remembered the monk lending her a CD that included his music, but she is not sure. The CD was stolen with her passport and laptop in London--so she will never know for sure. (Unless the monk writes her about it, but she is not going to ask him. It is not very important.)

he to the East and
she to the West —

she listened to the music. And now she likes Madonna's album *American Life* and hates that she does.

(When Harriet was in seventh grade
she went to an all-girls Catholic school

(she actually did this by choice

(which is sort of funny because the reason why she did this was so that she could get into a better college and when she did get into the better college, her family had spent a lot of their money sending her to the private high school and they didn't have the money to pay for the private

(and extremely expensive)

university that she was dreaming of and instead she went to the university that gave her a four-year, full-tuition scholarship.

Elizabeth Dembrowsky

At first, Harriet was very bitter because for most of her life, she had gotten everything that she had wanted — and to be so old and to be so lucky can make it very difficult to accept that "Hey, life isn't always going to give you want you want."

However, Harriet spent a long time being a brat

(but soon made very good friends

(like the geneticist/ molecular biologist and Katie[51]))

---

[51]Katie is/was grand. A book could be and should be written about her; however, this is not the one. Katie once said, "Harriet, I don't want you to write about me, because I think you have a warped perception of who I am, and I don't think I would like how you would portray me." Harriet was hurt by that, but decided to listen to her friend's wish and not write about her.

However, she is willing to share —"The Story of How Harriet and Katie Became Friends" only because it is such a good one and both Katie and Harriet have told the story so many times that writing it down is no crime.

The Story of How Harriet and Katie Became Friends

Week one of college, Harriet had already lost her Filofax (a weird organizer thing that had all of her ideas, I.D.s, and such in it) and was a mess, trying to find her way around the big, bad, urban campus and not bump into people and not get lost.

She was terrified, but tried to appear brave by dying her hair purple.

Week two of college, Harriet was visiting Boston College when her friend sat her down next to a girl that looked like a bossy-hippie, complete with black gorgeous, long hair and big, wide eyes. Harriet didn't like this girl one bit – she felt threatened. Her friend said in his "I'm friendly and optimistic and always see the cup as half full" way that because both Harriet and the girl with the black, gorgeous, long hair went to the same university, they should become friends.

Harriet felt very awkward because she didn't want to become friends with the girl with the black, gorgeous, long hair and definitely didn't want to be forced to be friends with her, but because Harriet is so often polite, she nodded quietly and quickly mentioned something about getting coffee. The girl with the black, gorgeous, long hair loved coffee and the two made plans.

Harriet and the girl with the black, gorgeous, long hair went out for coffee at the now defunct

(It is quite possible that the word *defunct* is misused in this sentence, but we will see what the proofers/copyeditor/or what-have-you's have to say.)

International House of Pancakes in Kenmore Square. They realized that they had a lot of cute things in common.

Things like:

- using the Violent Femmes song "I Like American Music" to try and ask someone to the prom.

- being from Massachusetts

- liking the books of Kurt Vonnegut

- being interested in Buddhism and Eastern philosophies in general

- having a friend named Bonnie who had a baby during high school.

and decided that maybe there was no force that made things happen, but that she was lucky to have such fabulous souls enter into her life at this point in it.)

But the biggest thing – was the strangest. Harriet and the girl with the black, gorgeous, long hair were very glad that they had gone out to coffee, and Harriet decided to ask the girl with the black, gorgeous, long hair for her email address. This was the beginning of the email address-based world that we seem to be in right now. At this time in the world, it was still quite a novelty and college kids loved to email one another. The girl said that her email address was *ghantous@bu.edu*.

Harriet started to act very strangely.	The girl with the black, gorgeous, long hair started to get nervous.
Harriet said, "Katherine, right? Katherine Ghantous?"	The girl with the black, gorgeous long hair answered, nervously, "Katherine, yes, but I go by Katie."
Harriet was starting to act very, very strangely. "And, you said you were from Walpole, right? Walpole, Massachusetts?"	By this time, the girl with the black, gorgeous, long hair was outright frightened. "Yes," she answered.

Harriet couldn't believe it. "I had a letter that was addressed to you sent to me three years ago. I hung it on my wall. You used to be a joke. I can't believe this. Katherine Ghantous from Walpole, Massachusetts!"

Harriet still had the letter in a box somewhere and weeks later brought it to the university so that Katherine, who went by Katie, could see it. After the PSATs, colleges began to send junk mail to students who scored well. Harriet and Katie were two of these students. Apparently, the person who sent the junk mail put Katie's letter in Harriet's envelope. Harriet kept the letter because she had a crush on a boy with the same last name; it later turned out that the boy was a cousin of Katie's and definitely not Harriet's type anyway.

After that the two girls decided that maybe Kurt Vonnegut had been correct and there was such a thing as a *carass* and that they each belonged in the other's.

and now is glad to have not gotten into debt over her degree and had the freedom to study whatever she wanted to and to run around the city of Boston, and sometimes Cambridge, and often Interstate 95, and not worry about trying to impress people that might give her a job when and if she proved to be the kind of person that they wanted her to be.

And – just to prove to her brother that she is "over it," she won't even mention the name of the college, because it does not matter.

> (p.s. though. It wasn't Harvard. Harriet isn't that smart and also didn't want to go to Harvard and also is pretty confident that she would not have much to offer that place.))

18

And so, the weeks went by and as the Thanksgiving holiday approached – Harriet decided to host a full, traditional dinner for the full class and was even to make him an Advent-friendly, Orthodox-approved version of the meal, complete with special gazpacho soup and vegan mashed potatoes. Her Spanish roommate laughed as Harriet, with a house full of hungry, expectant guests, idiotically opened the oven and pulled out with her BARE HANDS the small pot of milkless, butterless mashed potatoes that had been left there to remain warm before being served with the other, more traditional style.

He said to her in his gorgeous, Spanish accent, "Oh, it is love that makes you burn like this," and laughed loudly at her as he poured himself another glass of wine and watched her alternate jumping up and down blowing on her blistered fingers and running the cold tap water on them to help numb the pain.

But Harriet was convinced that it was not love that caused this – she and he were friends, just friends; she would repeat this new mantra to herself.

It was refreshing to be able to be so close to someone of the opposite sex and not have sex become an issue. Of course she found him attractive – that went without saying – that was what had drawn her attention in the first place. His thin frame was not what she was used to, but his height made him appear able to protect her – the need that every woman has but few will admit.

Usually, by the way, men want to be able to protect a woman, but very few can. In fact, I don't think any man can protect a woman but I think the want of him to do so and the want of her to have him able to do so is sweet. Women on the other hand do, in fact, protect men – a lot, actually.

In any case, his dark features and chiseled face were so exotic to a woman raised on Irish Catholic boys.

Okay, let's discuss the "Gay Issue."

Many people thought that perhaps the monk was gay – and was going to run away and hide in a monastery because he was ashamed. He wasn't gay. He was effeminate – very skinny and flamboyant and such, although he considered himself "a man" and had very strong feelings about what it meant to be "a man" or "a woman."

He had many traits that we in contemporary American society associate with gay men:

- Adoration of women like
    Madonna
    Marilyn Monroe
    Elizabeth Taylor
    Liza Minnelli

- Strong interest in fashion, including, but not limited to, the color pink and the pointy shoes that make women look like witches but somehow continue to remain popular.

- Flamboyant arm gestures.

- In his poetry he would refer to the object of his desire as male or female – and people were often confused by that.

The monk made many comments in passing regarding homosexuality and why he could no longer like Michael Stipe because of his admitted homosexuality.

Harriet tended not to fight with the monk about this issue, as she recognized that they were from two very different cultures and wasn't going to force him to accept her way of looking at things. She didn't think of herself as being "tolerant" or "accepting;" she didn't really think of it at all. People's lifestyles are their business and as long as they don't steal, cheat, lie, kill, or really annoy her, she let them be. In a way, she was bothered by the idea that one had to "tolerate" or "accept" homosexuality anymore than one had to "tolerate" or "accept" heterosexuality or chastity, for that matter.

She knew that he was not going to accept her point of view, so she didn't even try to force it. She even decided to be "Philosophically Orthodox" about it, in that she knew he knew how she felt; she was not going to try and "convert" him to her way of thinking; she would simply continue to live by her convictions and let her own life serve as an example of her beliefs.

Harriet learned a bit about Orthodoxy when she had thought that converting to his religion would mean that she and he would live happily ever after.

THERE IS NO HAPPILY EVER AFTER.
HARRIET DOESN'T KNOW THIS YET. DON'T TELL HER.

It is refreshing to be around someone who still believes in fairy tales this long into adulthood – "hope is a feather" – or something like that, according, at least to Emily Dickinson, another New England-born female poet, but one who Harriet does not want to grow up and emulate in poetic form or in lifestyle.

HARRIET DOESN'T EVEN LIKE WEARING WHITE.

The monk's discomfort with homosexuality made Harriet question whether or not he may indeed have been a latent homosexual but again, she continues to think that he was simply a very intense and free-spirited and smart and energetic man-boy poet/economist/monk-to-be.

*   *   *   *

A week before winter break, it snowed on campus. For the first time in over ten years, a white blanket covered the campus. Even if it lasted only for the better part of an afternoon, it was magical. Harriet was writing in her upstairs bedroom, glad that her landlord had found himself a girlfriend and would now spend weekends driving back and forth to Bath and leave Harriet in peace. She took an early afternoon break from her work, made a pot of coffee, and dialed into the university network system to check her email.

SNOW! In bold loud letters, the subject line from Leo stated the obvious. She smiled even before opening the email.

The Chinese girls are running around like chickens.
They love it as much as I do.
I think you must, too.

Harriet did love the snow. It reminded her of home.

*   *   *   *

The next afternoon she and he were again sharing coffee talk outside the post graduate computer room, interrupting one another with stories of childhood winters. Romania and New England seemed, for a few minutes that December day in the Western Midlands, a lot more alike than anyone had ever recognized.

19

A few words from The Monk:

First – "I will not sue anyone involved in the writing of this novel for libel. I will not do this for several reasons. First, I am too busy living in the monastery in the northern part of Romania, the region of Moldavia, the part the Russians did not get around to taking away from us. Too busy praying for the list of Harriet's friends that seems to grow each day; the list includes, but is not limited to:

+ Nikki Friedman's dad, who recently underwent brain surgery to remove a cancerous cyst.

+ Susan Turtz' son, Lance, who is dying of an awful, debilitating disease, not very unlike Lou Gehrig's disease.

+ Susan Turtz, who is a lovely lady deserving of prayer for her strength through this ordeal.

+ Patricia McNamara's dad, Roderick, who passed away two months ago.

+ Zina Zakari's father who passed away two weeks ago.

+ Tikva (Hebrew for hope) Mahlab's father who passed away one month ago.

+ Brenda Doucette, her husband, and their unborn child who Harriet thinks they should name Elizabeth, even if it turns out to be a boy.

+ Harriet's aunt, Andrea, who is suffering from all sorts of cancer.

+ Keshia Corbin who is getting ready to begin college and all the fun and work that it will involve.

+ Howard Rieger's wife, Tina, who is sick with cancer.

+ William Kapti's mother and grandmother.

"It is very difficult to get everyone's name right, especially as Harriet tends to email it once and never give me updates, so I never know what happens to these people – it's almost as if I am left to pray for fictitious characters or something, but I do it, because, as Harriet reminds me, it is my job.

"In addition to that, I run a writing center for young writers and help with a small but very active and always crowded church in Buchresti and seem to always have more exams that I am required to take; in fact, it seems as soon as I finish one batch, they have a new batch ready for me to start studying for – sometimes I think it is a bit ridiculous, but I don't say that aloud. In fact, these days, I say much less out loud. Difficult for me. I think the only person on the planet that this would have been even more difficult for is Harriet – but something tells me she isn't going to give it a try.

"Another reason why I will not sue for libel is because that is not the way we do things in Romania – we fight and yell and such, but suing someone about fiction seems a bit stupid to us – we often laugh at America when we read stories about silly court cases – my favorite is the woman who sued, and won if I remember correctly, McDonald's because she spilled the coffee on herself and got burned. Ah, we laughed a lot at that one. We also laugh, and this is not related really to court cases, but we laugh at the student at New York University who didn't want to pay for housing, so he just lived at the library. That is so funny to us, we bet we would like that guy!

"But the real reason I will not sue is because I once told Harriet that she could write whatever she wanted about me. I don't know why I said that; maybe I trusted her, I don't know. Maybe I knew she would write it anyway. I really don't know. Perhaps it is because I always wanted to read what she would write about it all. As much as she is a silly girl, I do sometimes like the way she looks at the world. I wish more people were like her – but maybe with more organization skills and with less to say....

"Do I love Harriet? Did I ever? Will I always? I am not going to answer those questions. I have promised myself to God for my life – a life of celibacy and prayer. Do I sometimes wonder why I made this promise?

Yes, I do. Do I sometimes regret this promise? Yes, I do. Do I intend to keep this promise for the rest of my life? Yes, I do.

"Who else will there be to pray for this growing list from Harriet? I never asked Harriet to fall in love with me. I get mad at her time and time again when she wants to go over details of what happened and why. As I wrote to her in one of my most recent emails to her – yes, I do have internet in the monastery, but it is very slow and I am only allowed to use it for ten minutes a day –

> *It is as if there are two cups of hot chocolate in front of you.*
> *If you can't have one of them, why would you throw the other away*

Sometimes I think that when Harriet would write me about needing to stop being my friend that she was trying to throw away the second cup only because she couldn't have the first one. I don't think it is fair that she blames me for this."

20

A few words from Harriet:

How utterly ridiculous! I never blamed him for anything, well other than being selfish and close-minded about things like his making me carry the soups while he got the salt and not wanting me to talk to the cute boy that picked up the dishes. I never blamed him for my feelings, all I ever asked was his understanding of why our contact became difficult for me. I hadn't planned on it either – I hadn't wanted to have feelings. They just happened. And different from any feelings I had ever had before – in fact, I was mad – not at him but at this whole G-d-Guy because I am convinced that He did it to me on purpose and I don't think that it is a joke – I don't think that messing up someone's heart like that is even remotely funny. Just because I don't believe in G-d is no reason for Him to be so spiteful towards me. I don't think it is a very nice thing that He did. And maybe He should be the one asking me for forgiveness – how about that for a change, Mr. Bigshot!

Really, the whole thing is an embarrassment and I want nothing to do with writing about it. I will stick to screenplays – I have two completed so far and one more treatment outlined and about a half dozen zygotes that have little more than plotlines ready to be expanded upon. I had hoped, when I was in Los Angeles this past November for work, to have had a chance to show them around.

I wrote up two separate treatments – one for a written (but to be honest in need of being rewritten) screenplay and one for which I have only written a treatment (while over the Labor Day weekend when I got a chance to go to the Berkshires for the first time) because I am afraid (because my friend Fran Sommers told me) that there is already a movie essentially like mine already in existence.

I held a reading that was mentioned previously, kudos to you, oh attentive, reader, Danny helped prepare salad that Nikki and I had stopped at the Greek grocers after tennis to buy "good Feta" for that would be washed down with orange juice and champagne that Cara and Eric brought, that would taste great before the donuts that Alison brought from the Polish bakery and that Amy and Aaron enjoyed before the reading.

In fact, I called all the friends and family on the West Coast that I knew and asked them and all the friends and family that had friends and family on the West Coast if they knew anyone who wanted to read my treatments. I even borrowed a little external drive – I don't know the word exactly but it is a little drive that you can put documents on from your desktop or email and take out and carry in your pocket and stick into another computer and use the documents from your desktop or email – I told you that I didn't know what it was called – that I had borrowed from work.

I even went so far as to use the free ten pages a day that the hotel provided for printing to make copies of both treatments. It was all pointless as I was too busy getting angry at what Bibi Netanyahu had to say and arguing over free wine with the COO/CFO (I was having the free wine, not him – I don't think he even drinks. I do know he likes cats and thinks I should get one and is not happy with the fact that I told him that the reason why I don't want to get a cat is because one of my biggest fears is to die alone in an apartment in New York City and have my cats eat me) over the fact that I think that Tzippi Livni does not need to change her haircut in order to become more respected. I defended Tzippi's physical appearance that I would describe only as "low maintenance" as being post, post modern (thought I DID NOT use that term) because "my generation" is not fazed by image any more and that her ideas were some of the best that I heard from that area in a while (I DID NOT use those words).

Too busy to find anyone to meet with other than my friend Wardell who took me to lunch at a great health food restaurant where we had Portobello mushrooms paninis and carrot and orange juice. I also went to dinner with my aunt Andrea and her friend who claimed "I am not a racist, but I don't like Muslims" and who to be polite about it all is also a very nice mother and friend and who paid for dinner at the fancy steak house and fish place that is the fanciest steak house and fish place that I have eaten in and where I saw two of my favorite women who work in finance and the head of I.T. and a few other people and felt strange to nod politely at them in this big restaurant.

Maybe I will return to the creative non-fiction piece *White Trash Intellectuals,* which Rose Dias thinks is funny or work on really getting the kids book, *The Girl Who Tried To Do Everything At Once,* that Brian Giblin and Jennifer (Pardi) Barr continues to tell me has potential, and on which Emily Mitchell from Charlesbridge Publishing in Watertown gave good but ultimately irrelevant feedback, and for which Mindy Wilson of Montana drew some, but not all, and painted illustrations, into the hands of some publishers or, at the very least, agents.

Maybe I will work on the play *love is the proof*, the one that Erin Smiley directed for Lovecreek and Thomas Michael Quinn did a reading of. I had planned to wait until March to start up again because March is when I will find out whether or not I won the Cullman Center Fellowship which means I could leave my job for one year and write everyday, which would be terrific.

I won't sit down and a write a book about why this man-boy monk poet broke my heart. I won't.

And did he really break my heart? I don't know. I asked Brenda about it recently. I was visiting my parents for a few days, recovering from the poverty (in money) and wealth (in experience) that New York City gives to me, when I went across the street to visit her. She is now six months pregnant. I think I am more nervous than she is – but she says, "Of course" when I ask her if she is nervous. In fact, she tells me, "Anyone who isn't nervous is stupid." But she is excited – I see the tired glow she wears. I see how she sometimes practices with her husband, cooing praises when he is out of earshot, praises like, "Oh, how nice of him to sweep the deck. I didn't even have to ask him a second time." I hear the coo and think of how nice it will be for Elizabeth, girl or boy, to hear from her or his mother when she or he accomplishes the fine feat of doing something as grandiose as taking a shit.

Brenda tells me that I did not love him – she says I am foolish for asking her this question and that if I need to ask her then the answer is most definitely no. I am not so sure. I think I may have. I think I created a version of him to love and loved that version – and that it was a fictional version, an overly romanticized one. I think perhaps I feel in love with the idea of falling of love. Is that such a bad thing?

21

leon–

so, i'm stupid and Polish and stupid and 'Harriet' and went crazy at about 7:30 am on sunday; however, i lived through it and slept on the bus most of the way. i did, however, take a nap at about 5 or so in the morning, right on the keyboard. as i was dozing off i kept thinking that someone was going to walk into the computer room and find me there, asleep in front of the screen, surrounded by bags of belongings: the homeless american grad student. but, on the bus my shut-eye really occurred.

    i had a really nice dream – you were in it, and i didn't beat you up, and you didn't seduce my best friend before giving me AIDS like in my awful nightmare – you and i were talking and giggling. then i woke up and turned to tell you something and then realized that you weren't there, that my bag of papers was, but you werent.

    i started to cry and the little cute ladies that complained about silly things all the ride, stopped for a second and looked at this strange girl crying. i pretended i had something in my eye and feigned falling back asleep.

    anyway, i've never been 'left' before. i've always been the one to 'leave' others. wow! it stinks. i should find everyone i've ever left and say 'sorry.'

    i'm trying to say i'm going to miss you, a lot. i will probably need 'de-programming' for a long time. however angry i will feel about meeting you, letting you 'rent out space in my brain for free,' one day i will be happy about it. i just hope my future husband won't mind my talking about some monk all the time. he'll have to be okay with it, i guess.

and so, if i'm mean to you or simply crazy the next times i see you, please understand that i'm – in my own weird way i'm trying to prepare myself. gloria told me – way back, when you upset me about 'rapture' and i realized that your opinion mattered so much to me and that i also realized that my many dreams about you are only dreams – that as long as i 'protected myself' there was no harm in our continuing a friendship . she probably knew that she was wrong, but she told me it was okay anyway, but cautioned me into being sure to recognize reality; i didn't listen to her caution.

one day, i'll publish love poems to a monk and definitely under a pseudonym, one i haven't even thought of yet. i'll probably do something slick by inventing a graduate student who finds these 'lost unsent letters from the 12th century' and rewrote them for contemporary times.

until then, this publisher/editor has work to do, including asking you to enter her Zabrosky@hotmail.com account and forwarding email from richard, christopher allen, m.freely and erasing the rest.

and send the translated poems, whenever you finish them, in devon.
which reminds me, the computer idiots here charged me an arm and a leg to 'resurrect' this old beast, and though i can't afford to make it a 'real lap top' and get the battery replaced to use it on beaches and hills and buses, it is working. the nice deborah's-dad's computer - though still used by me for printing - is all yours when you come down here, provided deborah and her dad say so.

– harriet

Leon–

Okay, a goodbye letter. I hate these. I know you think it isn't goodbye. In a way, you are right – in another way, you aren't (as it is with most things you say to me).

Thing is, in a while, maybe in a few years, maybe less, maybe more, I'll probably be able to write you – tell you silly things about 'finding G-d in my child's ear'

I don't know if you know of the Russian Communist who was 'converted' that way: he was feeding his daughter breakfast and looked at his young daughter's ear – and all of a sudden realized–that Something had to have created it. This couldn't have been an accident.

In high school, that story used to make me hysterical. In the back of my Religion Class I would put my hand up to my ear and wiggle it at my friend who was failing Biology (I later tutored her, she passed and now is a biologist – G-d help us all!) and make her laugh as I pretended that G-d was coming out of my ear, too.

I suppose I'll also tell you about the books I've written, the stupid critics who misinterpret everything, tell you about the house I finally find and how I've learned to grow sublime strawberries – or about Krakov and the fun in lonely living that I finally have found or about how L.A. isn't really that bad and how screenplays are fun to write.

Until then, I have to recover, de-programme, and heal this stupid thing they call a heart.

I'm not sorry though, that I let myself fall in love with you. It proved to me that I have a heart, that I can be hurt, that I'm not as analytical as I was trained to be. It also means that it can happen again, and with someone who isn't swearing himself to celibacy.

Initially, I really had planned to keep myself away from you, to finish my novel, to do the work I came here to do. But I couldn't do it. I didn't want to. Instead, I let you bug the ever-living shit out of me, and I learned to enjoy it. I'm happy for it all. It was beautiful in its own completely dysfunctional way.

When you annunced your plans to become a priest, I learned all about Orthodoxy and contemplated converting – I even have a friend that was teaching me how. But that wasn't right, it isn't right to the real people of faith of your religion – and – more importantly – I had somehow left you out of the equation. In my 'Harriet Way' I decided it all for myself.

I got over that – especially when the monk news came. And I have gotten over it.

I told the G-d that you believe in that I would stay your friend –until you left – that no matter how much I might not want to – that I would be patient with you and try to make your last months in the U.K. pleasant ones. G-d gave me a gift in the form of Deborah – someone much better than I at making the U.K. pleasant. I didn't have to break my word to Him, and I didn't end up having to do it all on my own.

I'm still searching for G-d, trying to keep my heart and soul open to Him and waiting patiently, trying my best to listen to His Rules in the meantime. Faith is a Gift, it isn't a decision – I will continue to disagree with you. Maybe it's part of a Western mind that you don't really understand, I dunno.

I'm glad I met you. Your energy and intelligence inspire me. I can hope again, in people, in creativity, in things that matter. I can appreciate those awful Hollywood movies and listen to pop music (on occasion).

I will miss you more than I dare to admit.

My friends are prepared for it – I've wrote them that when I arrive back there I will be a shattered woman and will need them to help me put myself together again; they better help me – they owe me that much. But, if they can't, or won't, I'll do it on my own – I always somehow have to anyway. I am glad to have things after 'this' that I can look forward to: nephews and marriages of friends and babies coming into my world and hopefully a new President and possibly a Ph.D. or a flat in E. Europe or a job here in the U.K. or care-taking for my parents as I become the weird spinster of Stoughton – growing grey hair and cultivating half an acre of daisies. Whatever it is, I'll get there.

And, if I don't write to you ever, please know that I couldn't manage it, that I had to cut off completely.

Of course, I probably will write – but I fear that when I do, I won't have much to say anymore. I'll find someone else to talk to, to tell my daily disasters to, to ask advice of, to listen to. I won't want to break that person's confidence, so my letters will be boring and trite, light-hearted and silly. Enjoy them if they come, because they will mean that I'm no longer looking for my Missing Piece – that I've found I was complete on my own, but that I have also found someone who has helped me realize that. Someone I can inspire and who can do the same for me. Someone to eat my cooking – which will improve –someone to hide the second bottle of wine from me when we have company over, someone who will learn to listen to me, only when I'm not talking – and someone to bring me flowers and coffee and chocolates and amber earrings.

Anyway, I wish you all the best in this life. I wish Andrew the patience to help you along. I wish your mom tons of Poetry lotion and perfume and a faithful husband. I wish your sister dozens of long-trunked elephants, and your dad happiness at home and in the world. I wish Romania to stand against war next time around – if there is one – and I wish the young poets there a chance to get beat-up by the critics of the English-speaking elites.

Take care of yourself.
May G-d Bless You,
Harriet Mary Angela Zabrosky

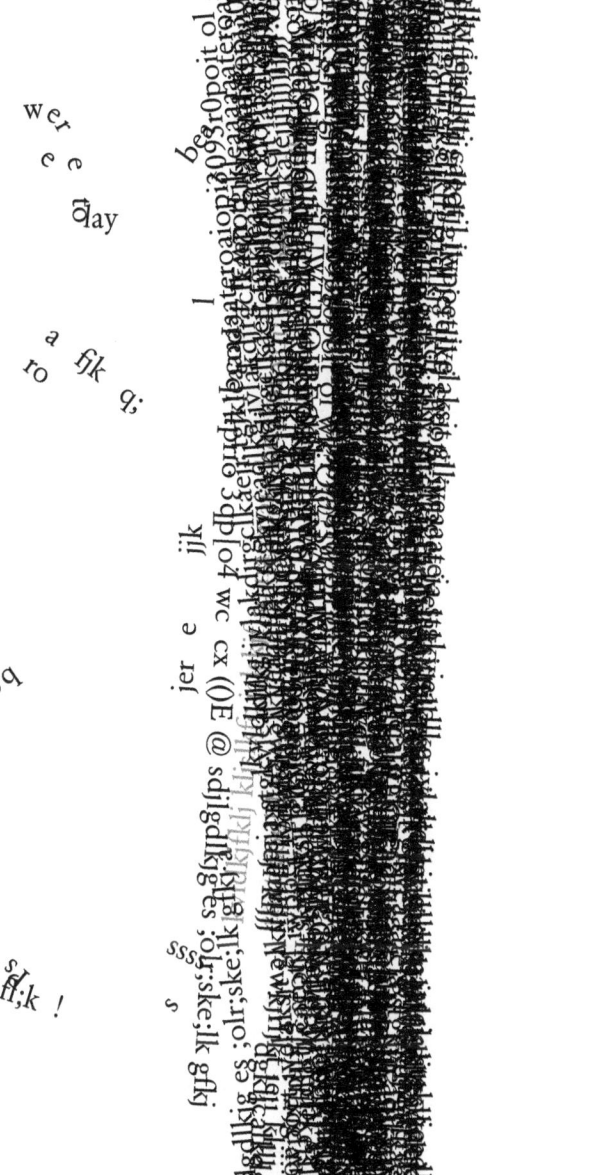

22

Before winter break, when the friends went their separate ways, Leo had written her the following:

I will be sure to pray for you this Christmas. It is my favorite time. I know that Easter is much more holy and important, but I do love Christmas more. I will pray for you.

Harriet felt insulted. They had already spoken on several occasions about religion, prayer, faith. She thought she had been clear that she didn't believe in any of it. How presumptuous of him to "pray for her" as though she were a lost soul who needed to have some sort of divine intervention to bring her back to the fold.

They were to see one another once more before boarding planes bound in very opposite directions. At that meeting he was more quiet than usual, and it took him a full half hour before he confronted her with what was troubling him. And, even then, he was not clear about it.

"In Romania, we pray for those we love. It is a special thing to do," he said between sips of the weak, black coffee.

"Praying for me is useless – but pray for those that need it, if you must."

My Monk

> At her answer, he went quiet and dropped the topic. The two walked with styrofoam cups in hand to the elevators to return to their work.

    One of the things that annoyed her most about the monk was that he was always asking her to write poems.

        (Harriet wrote poems when
        she was in grade school and later, in
        high school

            (during that adolescent stage
            of sadness, confusion, and
            rebellion)

        and even a little bit in college

            (but she never let anyone
            read them, because they were
            awful and embarrassing),

        but writing poems at the age of twenty-five

            (or twenty-six)

        did not interest Harriet.

She went to England to write a novel. A novel about a young reporter living on the island of Martha's Vineyard and her relationship with a reclusive native.

She did not go to England to write poetry. But she did. She wrote a lot of poetry. And, worst of all, eventually, she really enjoyed writing poetry.

Harriet

(like most people)

does not like it when someone tells her to do something that she does not want to do and then she does it and then she is glad that she did it.

Harriet

(like most people)

does not enjoy being wrong.

The monk was always trying to get Harriet to write about "uncomfortable" things and didn't like it that instead

Harriet wrote poems about Third Wave Feminism or writers that were dead or about paintings done by Edward Hopper or racism in 21st century America.

She knew she didn't want to write poems about herself because she knew that the monk would be in the poems and her feelings about him would be revealed. She didn't want to have feelings about the monk and definitely didn't want to write poems about it.

But, of course, she did. And no one has ever read them.

> (except her best
> friend Brenda
>
>> (the one that
>> got married)
>
> and they made Brenda cry.
>
>> (Brenda is the only one
>> of Harriet's American
>> friends that likes the
>> monk

(and she told
Harriet that
one day she
would like to
meet him

(which makes Harriet
very sad, because
Harriet never wants to
see the monk again))

and maybe it is because Harriet was able to share the good sides of the monk to Brenda and not always focus on the sexist or demanding things that he would say and not always focus on the fact that her heart was a mess because of the monk)).))))))

More words from Harriet

I sort of feel now is the time to defend myself. If you feel that I am any of the following:

- pathetic, for having tried so hard to be friends with someone that hurt me so much

- pathetic for focusing so much on it

- extremely self-centered and navel-gazing as to assume that anyone would care about it

you may be right.

However, every pop song, every movie, every novel

(well, almost every)

deals with these sorts of things. Being a human being can be pathetic, sometimes, especially when navel-gazing.

But I'm not interested in focusing on the war in Iraq

(though it was and continues to be very wrong and the U.S. government was wrong to try and enforce democracy around the world – especially when it can barely make it work at home)

or eighteenth century British class systems or science-fiction novels

(though I remain partial to Jane Austen, and Douglas Adams' science-fiction novel *Hitchhiker's Guide to the Galaxy* is a fantastic book, and I continue to love everything by Philip K. Dick that I come across).

I am interested in human interactions, misunderstandings, and again, why people fall for the wrong people.

So if you don't care about those things, I don't mind if you put the book down, or even return it. Chances are, I will have gotten so little for royalties, that I am still working another job and will not be financially crippled by your returning this book.

In fact, even if I find out about it, I will not be hurt. Not every book is for every person.

For example, *Catch-22*. No matter how many people tell me that it is a fantastic book

(like my close friend Mara

(who has a baby named Lyra

(and lives on Martha's Vineyard with her boyfriend Dave))),

I still can't seem to get into it to read it all the way through. I stop at different points, and put it down. Maybe one day I'll get through it, but for now, it remains a book that I just can't seem to read.

I hadn't meant for it to happen. I had planned for us to be friends. I had meant to fall in love with some rich British aristocrat or with a fellow-American who had left the U.S. for a while as well. I had not meant to fall for a man-boy who was planning on joining a monastery.

And still, I'm not sure why I did it. I used to believe that if you felt love, real love, you should never let it go. You should change your life and follow love, because that is the point of life.

I don't really think that anymore. I don't even know what love or real love is, and I definitely don't know how you can never let it go.

Maybe I liked the idea of the unobtainable and somehow knew that the man-boy was going to become a monk; I definitely knew that he was very religious.

Maybe I was jealous of his faith and thought that maybe he could give some to me.

Or, maybe I'm still trying to explain something that just doesn't make sense.

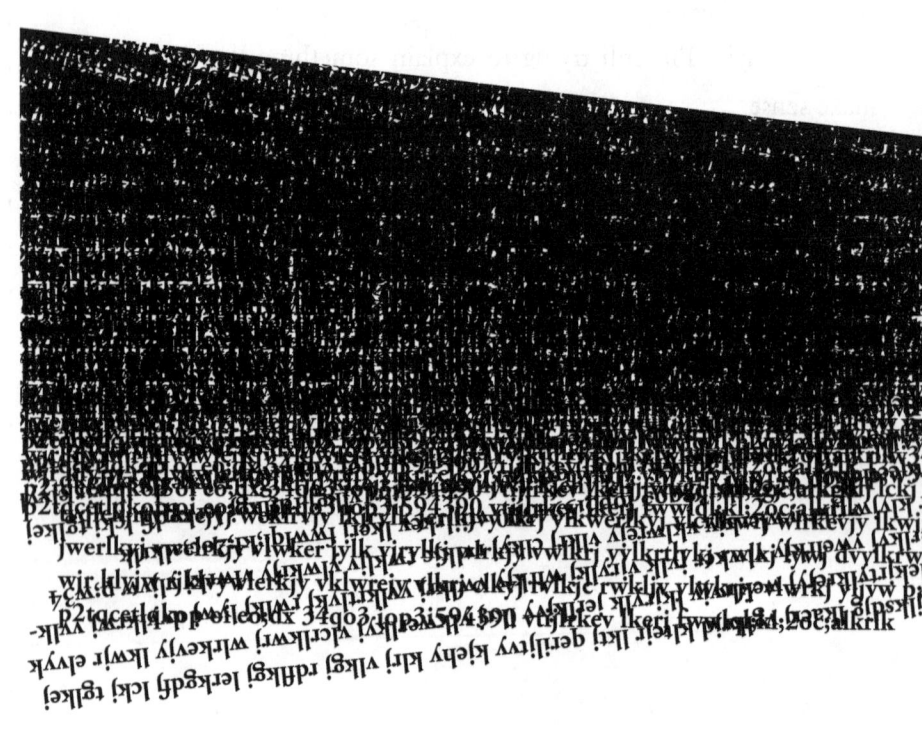

23

But she also wrote long-form poems that she called *Confessions* that were sort of letters to people in her life.[52]

---

[52]If you don't like poetry, I suggest, in fact, I insist, in fact, I highly insist, you skip this footnote. It is all poetry — very annoyingly abstract and seemingly at first, second, and perhaps even third reading without rhythm or structure.

It is Ginsburg's Beats meets urmanov's Utilitarian poets for a cup of bad Nescafe coffee at the Birmingham New Street Train Station to talk about why it seems that most revolutionaries are males and from middle class backgrounds and whether or not Condoleezza Rice is in love with George W. Bush and whether or not Laura knows and whether or not Laura feels bad for Condee and ever sets her up on dates with colleagues of hers from library school and whether or not Condee ever goes.

Elizabeth Dembrowsky

CONFESSIONS

a poem in july

Here where there is nothing
but inner smiles and bookstore women
the rudest in the world
and creamed teas for two
I am one
always on tour
bussing through Londontown
atop a red decked out bus covered with graffiti of S.T.D.s
laughing at the jokes told seven times daily

The biggest the brightest – the city better than Texas –
I, too, once spoke of third largest building on the planet
the second biggest department store.
Only the pizza is worth remembering –
forget Jordan and his women
the six wins celebrated in Grant –
we walked in as thousands walked out
throngs of fans marching in line, leaving dust of
beer cans - this couldn't have been America
it must have been Munich –

It had to be America where
we slipped past the coppers hiding our bottles of wine
to the jazz in Lincoln –
my sister, the best bad influence ever invented,
until she grew two of them
and converted into a model of matriarchy –
though I know she still sneaks,
I see the signs –
what being out on the porch really means –
the view is abysmal – a dirty yard next door –
the Chinaman has died and no blossoms grow
instead grass does seventy feet higher
than when Whitey would lend the push mower –

I used to push over the twelve square feet of land –
careful to avoid the beanstalks,
careful to watch my footing
for fear of death – or worse – eternal damnation.

He lived off those wafers – and hot dogs and beans
A ritual of eating, so carefully salted, so tenderly peppered –
and tea with two heaping spoons of sugar
from the tin I loved to play until he noticed
Reminding me 'children are to be seen and not heard'

He would smile –
I was twelve before I understood –
He never was a little girl.
He who never hugged –
When you tried, he would squirm –
How did his children get made?
How was he paired with a hydrant who kissed the mailman?
And demanded he eat cake from upstairs?
She never baked – but boiled water, dogs and food for the pigs –
And brought me to the barber shop and Bible school,
Washed me in the basement sink and dried my hair until it burnt
    under the heat of the YMCA hand dryer. She who swam miles
And bowled like a champ
And never swore – in front of me. She read her Bible, he his and I
    never knew
She was going to Hell. He only ever told my mother.

The carpenter who emulated Jesus.
The carpenter who said the rosary on his rocking chair in his sleep.
Tomatoes were always the first red and the juiciest
I hated them. Hated them hated them.

Only beans were mine –
I climbed the stalk to the sky,
Scampering away from chipped China and
Baseball games on Saturday afternoon.
There is no better place in the world for them to haunt than the rose
    bushes my sister tears up –
I tear up and remember how happy childhood was without bad
    movies, still color-blind, and perfect in the Sunday school
    where Peter was a rock of a fist and we never hid under bushels
    – No!
Neapolitan ice-cream after I was supposed to be sleeping on the thin
    bed higher than me.
I never had one single nightmare in that house.

The light is stronger than I am
It pulls me closer to you.
Above it swarms as moths
Tap a beat into its flame

Where is the watermelon?
And the seed fights?
The firecrackers to make us forget the falling bombs?
The corn on the cob buttered to perfection?
What celebration have I missed?
Who do I miss?
Who misses me?
Where is my country?

Elizabeth Dembrowsky

What has it done?
Has it fallen –
Asleep?
Has it fallen?
Has it fallen
Yet?
Why do I care so much?

My friends are gone, I want to go –
He says he'll cut my legs.
He says he'll nail the wings on.
I know they won't stay.
My skin will resist
Reject the metal in my shoulder blades –
Push the aliens away
And tell me I need to climb the trees:
Flying will never work for me –
To where it bent in the undergrowth –
I am stuck here hiking the Appalachian Trail of Tears to China.

Who will cry when I die?
Will you?
I say I don't want you to –
I want you to sing and hold a party to out do Janice
But, really, I want wailers and the best-breast-beating, be Jew and
Muslim mothers whose sons have blown up –
Be sad, rail, because you won't know either if I've made it –
If I doubt, please hope that Nietzche was right,
Because if I don't – I don't want to burn –

My skin only partly olive –
This Slavic epidermis prefers mild temperate climates,
Except in summer, when twelve days worth lead me to jump in lakes
The locals say is too dirty. I'm too dirty. I need to be baptised
Again and again and again –
Especially if I want to make it.

There is a crack in my skull
It is where my sanity left me –
Where the bug bit down and grew and grew
And through me – made a home –
In me – that bug in me – forever rotting-
Forever there. As original as sin as everlasting
As heaven. Rotting there in the crack in my skull
Letting the light in, adding dopamine to my over-tanned
Temporal lobe – it is coming to tell me that the synapses have
Stopped firing, they've asked for the night off –
There is a movie on the telly that they've been dying to see.
They leave me empty as a stomach of a bulimic –
Forty minutes after eating the cookies and cakes and cheese left out
As a temptation. Avoid it – avoid it all. Empty mind in Buddhist circles.

My Monk

The therapist gave me a ride in her car and drove like a maniac
I recognized her
I was supposed to grow and be as stressed as she is,
Scheduling Swiss meditation trips between sessions.

I laugh in the back seat and feel my wet legs – the rain soaked through
The swans are still alive – barely – just like me.
All like me – ugly and grey like the skies of England.

The hills of Devon are green and the sheep stutter and I hate them.
They complain all day and extra hard and extra loud when I
Waltz by – on the fastest walk the countryside has ever seen –
Swinging my arms and my hips with a smokers' cough
Up the wrong path
Avoiding the dogs and the nettles
In no particular order. Racing the sun along the Dart –
In and along until the cows scare me into stopping
Resting here with Atwood or Plath under my armpit,
Roll myself over and a cigarette to smoke along the Dart
In and out of the words
I'm picking up where they left off
A new wave.
A Third Wave.
A tiny surf along the Dart.
The sun has fallen behind the sheep, setting them on fire,
I wander back
Past Mary's perfect hands and grass I chew, no longer afraid of cows,
Moving along the Dart back to a house I've dreamt of since five
And make myself a cup of tea
And build a dream.

Baroque

A rough pearl:
a clumsy grace
all heart and turmoil

Tolstoy and Christie on a rope swing
debating the merits of following form

So this is goodbye
on a rope swing over the Atlantic
the one that warmed me and let me dream
of a life
I forgot after the waters cooled

Tolstoy and Christie on a rope swing
Lecture the Catholic with a Protestant Work Ethic
    The mule that wishes to be a wasp.

This funny place where criticism stems but action withers
and wilts as basil leaves unwatered for days
wilted basil leaves on Polish strawberries

Don't tell them
all strawberries will always be Polish
always
and forever
served with Russian black market cigarettes
eaten unwashed and swallowed whole without clotted cream
without sugar and spice and everything nice

You cannot go back
to a place you have never been

You can try

You can try to
drive on into the east

The sun won't rise for another day

You are safe to fly until it does
down highways that connect
City Lights to Deli Houses
and stop to visit
a cow and a college and a coffee shop that closes
at midnight
just in time for scary men in slow cars
to challenge you
to
play tough

play deaf
hold hands
and run like hell
past derelicts
singing of playgrounds and fears and futures
that will pull you apart
of futures you fear you promise will never come
to days when tears and laughter float over space
that was never to exist

Five-winged mansions and giggling girls drinking tea and vodka

go where there is darkness and bring –
your cult with no leader

The leader cries at night
far from –
and them
and the King Street Pepper Posse
that would later cry after tapas
but before made tapes of Swedish Keroac
and laughed at furniture
and laughed at air conditioning
and drank cheap beer until your blood was drunk
your ears burned in the heat of the F.B.I. before the attacks –
they killed the man with paranoia
who told you to steal the book
after levitating
the Pentagon
you visited with a victorious sign of peace before the attacks
during the time when your biggest concerns involved creative ways to
stop educating dictators and picking favorites that favored conspicuous
something or other
and Ollie arming Contras
against Contras against Ollie
and Albright's economics killed six million
or was it seven
women and children and women and children – the first to go
until later
after attacks and holes in the sky and holes in the ground of a state
where the highway never ends
but meets a guard rail at fifty-five
and holes in the Pentagon
you visited with the I.R.S. tax attorney at your back

You asked no questions
and felt that you were being watched
only b.c. that is how the movies showed it

This was a movie – it had to be a movie of an acid dropout on
Ninth Avenue

Elizabeth Dembrowsky

telling of the Apocalypse
as he walked into the fog and kicked the trash bin at the Muni stop
where ad campaigns made you smile
about a war against Seattle
that only cost billions of dollars –
of den mom calling her wayward son
to ask about his talented younger
of an overly emotional aunt asking
if you had spoken to your sister
of speaking to your sister
strong and crying over the line about leaving the gym and seeing
it fall
seeing
it fall
from four miles above
and everyone who had entered the apple was dead in your mind
and you fought back by crying in Radio Shack and hating the West –
Coast for being three thousand million miles away from everyone and
every hole and every brave good thing
you still believe –
in
fighting back
by buying a brand new radio
and crying in the department store with Brokaw having not slept for days
and Nader spoke and warned of Afghanistan preaching as Jesus
a hippie said
and you knew
they wouldn't listen
to you or to him or to the man holding his four-year old baby-child in
his arms
she holds a teddy bear in your mind's eyes and she cries about bullies on
the
Playground of Democracy.

Glor

Beans and toast
No bean town

Beans and toast
And tea with cream

Coffee with milk
And bottomless refills
Setting stomachs on fire
And fights in the booth
About Nietzsche's hidden love for Jesus
And our secret fears of dying alone
And childhoods
That weren't always happy
And adolescences that never were
Where we were
When you hid under a desk
Those mushrooms had the cost of living real low
Those mushrooms we hated
As anchovies and tomatoes
And olives I love
You and rain puddles and the nights we cried
Because evil chemists didn't understand what we were trying to do
What where we trying to do?

We didn't understand
Anything
And now we still don't
But we know it now
We did learn something
The thirty thousand dollar apple
We got free
Running from security guards and squirrels to the park at midnight
Where the glitter twins sang Guns N Roses
And we humoured them and bought them booze
And never gave them sex – they knew better than to ask –
Until later – lifetimes later
Where men coughed out AIDS dying in the place that gave me fleas
The bartender had a kind smile but worked against me
And for him
And I told the truth
And he thought he could deal with it

24

Is he still alive?
He owes me money
And promised me a fishing boat and a house in Greece
Never thinking I would make it here

Consider this a postcard.
I'm here
Where is he?

Is he still alive?
Still covered with fleas
The best kiss I never wanted
My moral high ground, you disapprove
I'm not sorry
But you are
Sorry that I'm not

Coffee and hangovers – I paid for both
A bagel and orange juice and
Objectivism

He searched too
In different flea-ridden flats across America
We paid him to
Search for something
We knew he wouldn't find

Is he still alive?
Living in the penthouse with wooden floors in the East Village –
Dylan-style my ass
My ass is grass
And I have no more money
I gave it all to him

Is he still alive?
This is the credit card company calling

My Monk

This is the W.T.O. and NAFTA and the government
we object to
objectivism

                          I was supposed to write a novel or five
                          And I can't even get a line of poetry
                                          Out
                                     of here –
                                Can you hear me
                              From across the pond
                         I hear you crying on the line

                                    Give us something
                                      To believe in
                                  We need to believe
                                       In something
                     We can't define or deny or decide

              You will baptise your children, you hypocrite.
                                        I will too.
                                   Will we tell them?
                              Or become our parents?

                                Our parents believe –

                                         I believe
                                         In you
     Splashing in the rain and running across Storrow at dawn
                            And me puking into the Charles
                            I made it cleaner you know
The Dali Lama jumped in and they took him straight to Mass General

               You and Plath worked there – don't get any ideas

                                       You won't –
                            We are in for the long haul
                         No matter how much it hurts
        To carry the world on our backs and in our hands
       Nursing the Velveteen rabbit with X's over his eyes

                                  My people are mules
                Yours are sacred cows and dentists' wives
                          Teaching piano fortissimo
                                Yelling at maids
                               We cannot afford
                            Much in this world
       Studios in Greenpoint and bus rides to kingdom come

                              They are all the same
                          from the Yucatan to Lomza
From Chinatown to Chinatown with chickens and discount rice paper

Elizabeth Dembrowsky

Remember Ginsberg?

I am still smoking
Slowly suicidal –
I'm not perfect –
Yet – my dear – yet-
Don't tell the others
I enjoy romantic comedies
and am tired of crying for starving children in Africa
Sudan last week and in two they will turn over Iraq

When will we learn to leave alone?
When will I learn?
To leave?
Myself in one place?

I want to stop spinning and running and lay down and wait for 500 years to pass

I want the ulcers to heal
My mind

Leenda

Tea and old ladies:
A shared dream
Since five

The freeze pop and the hot-as-hell afternoon
Where we kissed Saint Francis
And knew the dog would never tell the tale
Never tell McCarthy
That we with hands over mouths
Made-out under the pine trees
Covered with sap
Picking blueberries that bit back
And scratching arms with thorned black ones as well
And stirred red hard bulbs of poison
As all lost children did and do and forever shall
Til kingdom come.
It will be done.

Pink paint with too much white
Scared away the little boy
With teeth like a rabbit
And a rabid sister who –
Whose mother was the first
Who made me stare at Jesus with thorns on his heart

Whispering *don't* before my lines –
Why did we have to say them?
To identify with them?
To not let it happen again?
It happens everyday –
Little hitler's wash their hands
And run away to baptise themselves
In frigid water of ketchuped blood
And run away to hills of music
And sounds of parrots I need to kill
Little hitler's wash their hands.
Under lights the stain remains

At five:
The thorns in the heart
The universal guilt.

I want to be a little hitler and wash my hands
His feet my face
My body stripped to nothing by truth
Never wanting truth
Never wanting me
Tell me tell me the truth
The universal unarmed truth

Elizabeth Dembrowsky

Lime rings around waken me to a world
I am not apart of
I will be a part from you
And five year olds
Who knew they would
One day drink tea
If only over the telephone:

How is the weather?
And the tropical plants?
Is it true Hemingway was gay?
That must explain the cats.
How many do I have?

I'll tell you no lies
You hated my grades
I your perfect skin
Inability to hide an emotion
Loyalty to something as silly as the evil capitalist that ran the lemonade stand
Fists that struck at me when I sent you home

You had no choice
With the first swear
And the first kiss of Saint Francis
Black, loud, and rated PG 13
You were mine
Love at first site

How many times have I left?
Does it get easier?
Tell me the truth.

It is all I've ever wanted.

I can't handle it.
I can't handle you
Handling him
Handing me over
To this-
To this life of solitary confinement
Of fast cars and loose morals
And European coffee
Served in porcelain cups.

Where is the tea?
And the old ladies we shall become?
Your kids will call every Sunday
I will cry into my computer
The fifth one they stole
No – I will never learn

My Monk

Some Russian wrote about it
They were always the best.
Don't tell McCarthy
Anything –
Tell me everything.
Tell me even things I don't want to hear.

My ears are blocked by sounds of poetry
Fictive words to escape to.

I hate them still
These who laugh at us
For trying
For believing.
For fucking things up.
We fucked things up.
We need to stop.
We have to stop
If only for the children I will never have
If only for them.

Rabid rabbits damn catholics
Heart of thorns
Stop the bombs.
Stop the cardinal that flew away to Rome
To run from bars he deserved
Tell us what to do
After screwing little boys.
What bible have you read?
Is it different from mine?
I can't listen to you
Read.
I won't tell you what's wrong.
What's wrong?
You are
You are wrong.

I need tea and to be an old woman
Already purple, already talking to myself
When you aren't here
To tell me not to
To tell me to wipe my sleeve
And to take the snots from my eye

Five years to wait until small islands that
Raised your mother
Till she ran from the convent
To America
To convert into
    what –
Into a dream of a blue house and a big screen t.v.

And a red cooler to take to the beach where
Your dad had the first video camera in the whole wide world.
And we fat and never lazy eating popsicles
In the sand castles that I told you how to build
And driving in the car tired and salted as lobsters
I was too scared to eat.

Waking in the night from hell
Walking you home and walking me home
Talking for hours in the direct center of the trip.
We calculated it –
Justice always the american way
Our american way
The only way we would ever have
What happened to that
What will we tell the children I'll never have?

Bootney

The albino "n"
With so much soul
And too much salt
Who swam at the Y
And hiked the seven flights of stars
To watch the sun fall into the Pacific
We dreamt about since high school
Driving across the country

I made the movie.
It is in a box somewhere
In someone's basement or attic or trash bin
The soundtrack of our lives
For that one week
Of knowing the beatniks were spoiled men
Who refused to accept responsibility
For the children they left
Across amerika we drove
Falling in love with old men in gas stations
Geizers
And geysers
On the strange planet
We landed on
The strange planet
Where Iowan farmers and Japanese tourists
Talked non-stop.

You never take me seriously enough
To stay angry.

Of all of them you deserve it most
And me second.
So it's my turn.

I'm not supposed to ask
These silly questions keep me up at night
As caffeine in builders tea.

Your heart is almost as big as your ass.
Mine is smaller
Only because
I can no longer afford ice cream and cheese and to drive in a car.

Your heart will stop if you don't stop
Your salt intake
Into the ocean to swim the length of the pool of 19th Avenue
Where the crazy old lady always let us in for free
Our timing was perfect.

Elizabeth Dembrowsky

Swim the length of the ocean
Speak German
Tell me about *Brothers*
I did read the *Underground*, you know, I wrote for it, too.
And gave them money to make t-shirts to fight any system that approached us
As we walked alone at night along 'nameless streets in the name of finding...'
I thought he was a poet – and never told him that.
The amusing muse to a room full of tortured something or others
You always cried when you drank and would always try to run away
Where were you going?
Can I come with you?
To Berlin?
Now that the wall is down
And up on the Gaza Strip
Can we walk naked through the Gaza Strip Mall and boycott Starbucks?
We will make them all so angry
They will forget to shoot each other
And shoot us instead
– I always wanted to be a martyr –
Singing soulful church songs
In memory of Aretha and Martin
Rosa and I have the same birthday
So guess where on a bus I sit?
Where ever there is a seat
Next to you
In a tiny car
That took us across the wonderful land and horrible government that we made

Will you land on these shores before I leave?
For a newer old continent?
Will you leave him – that boy who stole your-
Will you leave him in the Everglades and let the alligators eat him in the Everglades?
Let's eat alligators again – it must be somebody's birthday, somewhere.
Or is there already another strip mall along Gaza?

    We were born old and will die immature
    There are worse Fates to Muse about.

25

Her mother found it strange that Harriet spent so much time in front of the computer that week she was back in the United States.

"Why be so anti-social, you have so little time home with us?"

But Harriet could not easily be convinced to separate herself from her writing. Her novel was taking a stronger form and as the course was already a third of the way completed, she was aware that she needed to use her time very well if she wanted to complete her goal of returning with a completed text: *The Islanders* was to be her breakthrough novel and no time could be wasted on creating the final copy. But there was another reason as well – she missed him. She thought that writing connected her to him.

On Christmas Day itself she received an email from him – it seemed so odd for her. In her mind Romania was a backwards country of haystacks and vampires, corrupt bureaucrats and dirty peasants. Internet accessibility seemed out of place in this second world country.

It snowed on Christmas Eve, and I lit a candle for you. I talked a long time with my Father and have made some very important decisions. I cannot wait to tell you of them.

> *My friends, I have two of them, are already tired of hearing me talk about you all the time.*
>
> *Lots of good love to you,*
> *Leo*
>
> She excused him for lighting the candle for her – she held some bit of Christmas spirit within and thought of these three beetle-obsessed poets sitting in a smoked filled café in Bucharest yelling at one another animatedly. She thought of her name coming up in their conversation, and smiled. What sorts of things was he saying about her to them?
>
> She herself had written home over the last three months group letters where she would refer to him only as "The Romanian" or even "The Romanian poet" but never by name.

    (She also likes that the director of her writing program gave her nice compliments on the poems – and coming from a British person

        (not known for giving out compliments so freely the way many Americans do

            (in fact, if compliemnts were water, a

lot of people in
England would
be thirsty and a
lot of them
might even die
of dehydration))

this meant a lot.)

In fact, she would one day again like to write poetry — but hide them in pop songs. Harriet would like to write pop songs, not the Britney Spears kind, but the R.E.M. kind.)

When they arrived back on campus after the break, she noticed a difference in him. He was the same fickle, needy, demanding Leo she had known, but there was a resolve in him that she had never seen before. When he spoke to her he would reference the future as if it were a set plan, something already predestined. Whatever it was, Harriet didn't like it. She thought if she simply ignored it, maybe this new oddness would go away. It didn't.

His resolve increased and combined with a more solemn attitude, almost lecturing at times. He who would before have been the first to suggest a break, now treated her offer of candy as a silly, distracting nuisance and would wave it and her away with a dismissive hand.

Although this hurt Harriet, she never expressed this to him. Instead, she turned inwardly to wonder at both what had brought about

> this change and why it bothered her so much. During this time Harriet began to recognize symptoms in herself of deeply caring for him. She convinced herself that this was under her control, that it was the natural progression of a man and a woman who get along so well, find one another attractive, and spend so much time together – but that the two of them could prove everyone wrong. They could be friends, just friends. She would repeat this mantra to herself every night before she went to sleep, but when the alpha waves took over, something else would happen.

She asked the monk to pray for her cousin. She figured he would because both the monk and her cousin were Eastern European.[53] Harriet didn't write in the email to the monk that her cousin felt that the Church and that sort of thing was a load of bull. He had seen a lot in his life – Nazism, Communism, being poor and unappreciated in the land of opportunity and heartache and headache and all sorts of ache. He didn't believe in organized religion, and, although Harriet never asked him, she was pretty sure that he didn't believe in G-d either.

(This cousin did not take kindly to Harriet's criticisms of U.S. Foreign Policy and of the war in Iraq. He had been in Iraq and in Israel and in Palestine and in Libya and in a slew of other places during the Second World War.

---

[53]Actually, Poland may or may not be in Eastern Europe. Many people consider it to be in Central Europe and especially as Poland was accepted into the E.U., it isn't a country/culture that is considered to be as "eastern" as Harriet tends to think it is.

It is likely that Eddie thought Harriet both spoiled and naïve.

It is also likely that Harriet's Uncle Paul, who was a fighter pilot in Vietnam and made a career for himself, and a pretty good one, in the U.S. Air Force that culminated with him retiring at a ridiculously young age, perhaps 50, with the dream he had set out for himself: to be a man of independent means – thought Harriet both spoiled and naive. And he is, what with a house in Germany and a house in Florida and a boat and a camper and a Vespa and one or perhaps two Saabs and two Scottish terriers – a man of independent means that is. We still hope that Harriet will get married one day, and we doubt that her parents will approve of a large wedding, and therefore will not pay for a large wedding, and we know that Harriet recently has spoken about a very large guest list to her wedding because there are so many people that she wants to be there when she promises to spend her life with just one person. What does this have to do with accusations of naïveté and being spoiled? A lot – if you plan on hitting up a childless uncle to pay for your large wedding.)

Harriet wrote a poem about the car trip across Poland to go to the funeral. The poem is part of the newer work that she recently started writing. She jokes that it is Pop Music Poetry as it often has a chorus and several verses.

(Remember Harriet likes Michael Stipe-ish pop music versus Britney Spear-ish pop music.)

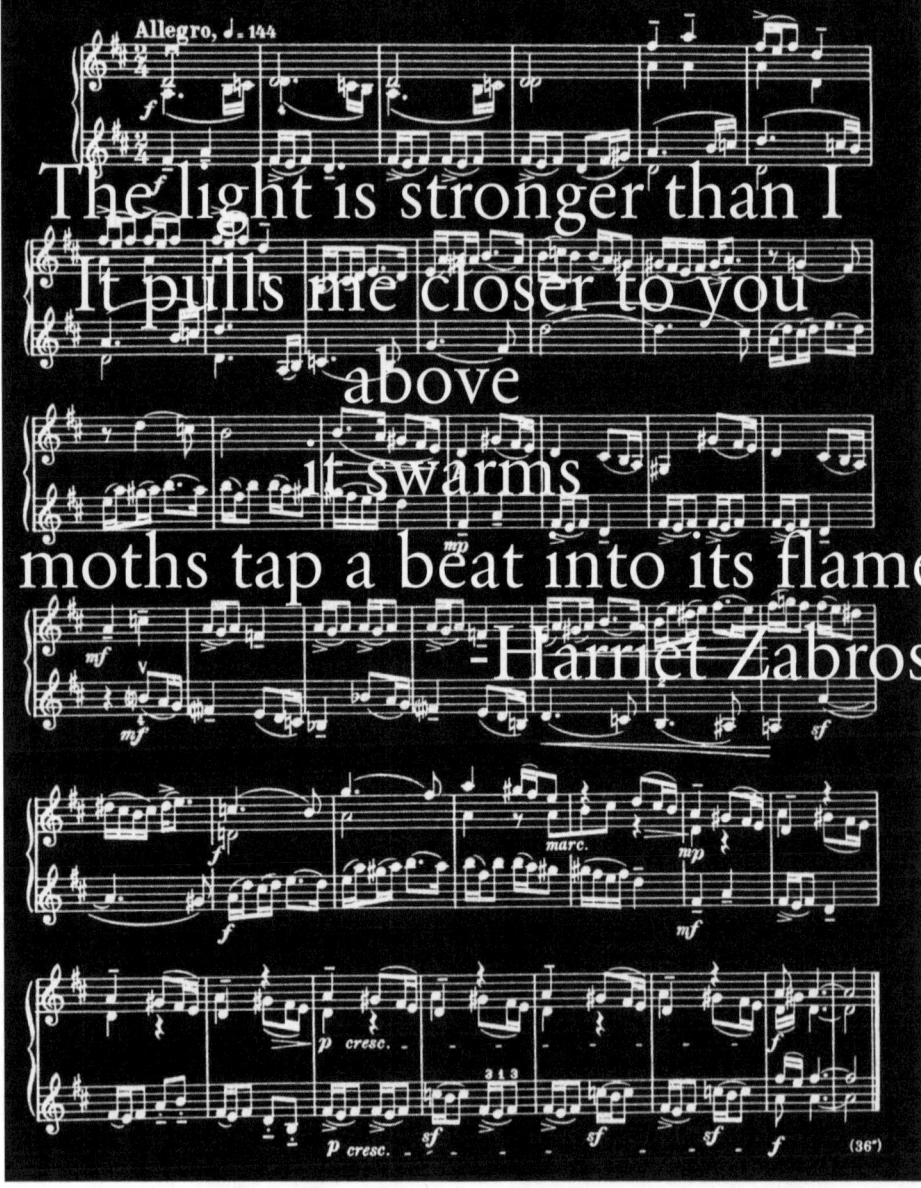

26

Driving Tips

Trekking tractor tread-marks[54,55]
Peasantland of Ikea sales[56]
Paprika sunset and dirt-cheap smokes[57]
        Son of a gun[58]
        Son of a gun
        Where you gonna run?[59]

Gorgeous haystacks at traffic stops[60]
American Gothic in Torun[61]
To run back to black *babushkas*[62]
        Son of a gun
        Son of a gun
        Where you gonna run?

Seven-year-old poets[63]
An economics professor
Who sits in the wood with your picture[64]
        Son of a gun
        Son of a gun
        Where you gonna run?

Coleslaw conversations[65]
With *herbata* and an old smiling woman[66]
Who kisses three times
She loves, loves, loves you
        Son of a gun
        Son of a gun
        Where you gonna run?

Polish hip-hop pit stops[67]
Fries and a Coke with every developing smile[68]
Faked with ketchup, served for zlotys[69]
Before back to Western sunsets[70]

Elizabeth Dembrowsky

Engineered road accidents:[71]
Pin-wheels for grown ups[72]
Driving Mercedes[73]
              Son of a gun!

---

[54]In high school, I had a wonderful English teacher named Mrs. Atkinson, who I thought was a witch. I sort of still think that she might have been some sort of pagan – or I wish that she was; my high school teachers were all so nice and boring and mostly Catholic and very honest and very upright – it would have been fun if the smartest of them (well, tied for smartest -- my Calculus teacher, Mrs. Fidler, was pretty bright (and Polish, too!)) was a pagan. Anyway, she was terrific and almost everyone hated her – because she was hard – all good teachers are. I remember one day getting very upset about her precise analysis of something or other, possibly *Return of the Native* but maybe one of the *carpe diem* poets. I whispered to a classmate about it – I did A LOT of whispering in high school. I then raised my hand and began a discussion about "How arrogant it is to assume that we really know what was in the mind of a particular writer?"

It is about that time that I started the *Live Poets Society*, a knock-off on the movie *Dead Poets Society* which was the first PG 13 movie I was allowed to watch. My movie and television watching were VERY censored when I was growing up.

We used to meet outside at lunch behind the rhododendron bush – now that I am older, I can smile widely at that little nerd. We moved our meetings to *Friendly's*, the chain restaurant, as soon as we had cars. We would write "jelly bean" poetry – poems that meant absolutely nothing, but that you could try and find meaning in if you were assigned to in a high school English class. Much later in life, after college, actually, while living in San Francisco, I went to an art exhibit that showed the works of the Dadaists and realized that those folks had beat those little fifteen and sixteen year old girls in plaid skirts to the chase. But there is a beauty in knowing that you aren't original.

For some reason, I am the only one that remembers doing this, but I know that I didn't make it up. In fact, on a visit to my parents' house a year or two ago, I found some of the "jelly bean" poems. I'll have to find them again and show them around and prove that I wasn't making this up.

In any case, for this poem "Driving Tips" I will provide a very explicit "key." In fact, the title itself was originally "Driving Across Poland," but I realized that the title was very banal so I changed it.

[55] Okay, line one. Alliteration. Alotta alliteration. (well, not really a lot, but enough). Trekking – to move across. Tractor – double meaning. Poland has lots of tractors, farm ones. Taken together with the third word, Tread-marks, it refers to the eighteen-wheelers that were so overloaded with goods that their tires left marks in the highways. When you drive across the country you have to decide to either drive within these huge divots, avoid them completely, or else risk getting a flat tire. In Germany, this doesn't happen because they are very regulated, some would say over-regulated, and only certain vehicles can carry certain weights.

[56] This one is easy. Peasants – Poland is/was full of them. My Slavic roots were peasants, though there was a chemist in there as well. Ikea sales – is a quick quip on globalization. My hometown doesn't even have an Ikea, yet – they are negotiating to get one, but rural western Poland does.

I also worked, and this probably need not be mentioned, to use repetitive vowel and consonant sounds to go for a certain rhythm within each line. But that stuff is boring. Plus, I don't want to give away all my secrets, do I?

[57] Paprika is often used as a flavoring (and really as a decoration) on traditional dishes and is the color of the sun when you are driving across the country in August. Cigarettes are very inexpensive as well.

[58] Okay, so this one is really random. The Polish cousin, who is still alive and lives in my hometown, would often say "Son of a gun" for no apparent reason. It must have been a phrase that he picked up from the British or American soldiers he had met, I don't know. But I do know that he would often say it.

[59] This means exactly that, "Where you gonna run?" You give "Driving Tips" but to where? Or Harriet gives them, or the girl who went to Poland, or the narrator, or the author, or the footnote taker or the "poet in denial." Wow, this can get a bit confusing, but I think you are smarter than the Europeans believe, and you can figure it out, idle reader.

Or if you are a European reader, then for sure you are idle, and for sure you are smart enough to understand post-post-modernism, right? Even if you can't produce/develop blockbuster movies or sweet and sour sauce as good as McDonald's, you are very good with theory and literature and such, right? Don't let me down, I have my faith in you, and might even leave my homeland when and if I get pregnant and deliver my little baby or babies on your soil to give them a chance at the European citizenship that I am without.

Elizabeth Dembrowsky

⁶⁰This is a cute story. I rented a car from a place in Hamburg and convinced my German-American friend to come with me. She cannot drive, but I thought the company would at least make for a fun adventure.

At one point, the traffic was stopped for a full hour. There was some weird construction going on. I got bored and got out of the car. Now, I can be an annoyingly optimistic person. This was one of those times. I pointed at a haystack and started marveling at how beautiful the design was, how "my people" can make gorgeous art from such simple things, *yada yada yada*. My traveling companion was not buying it. She actually might have threatened me over it – saying something to the effect of, "Harriet, if you don't stop talking about the haystacks, I'm leaving." Where was she going to go? I don't know. Neither did she. However, I have this beautiful photograph of her, looking very "Polish" actually standing there on the side of the road. If I remember, maybe I will bring it along on the book tour and show it to you.

⁶¹Everybody knows that *American Gothic* painting, right? You know, the one of that sad-looking, skinny couple? The pitchfork? Yeah, I knew you knew it. Anyway, I saw this beautiful couple – they were so lovely I almost cried – working together in a field. Because I remain "devastatingly single," I get really, really jealous of old couples. Anyway, they were so adorable. And we drove through a town/city called Torun. The place, however, is most likely pronounced "tor un" and not "to run," but let me make a little pun every once in a while, will ya?

⁶²"To run" refers both to the place, Torun, and to the idea of running to the past – sort of a reference to the earlier poem that discusses coming "back to a place you have never been" and because travel is the theme of the poem, running is allowed. Back, black, babushkas is a bit of the ole alliteration, a continuation of the backwards movement in time, and a reference to funerals. Funny thing is, I pulled what I consider to be a "Madonna" move, the pop star and not the religious icon, not that I know that she ever did this; however I can completely see her doing these sorts of things in England all the time--i.e. assuming that Europe has not changed from what you learned about in grade school. Even in rural, eastern Poland, women do not all wear black babushkas, those bandanas for your head, to funerals – except of course if they are a 26-year-old woman named Harriet from America. In which case, they spend twenty minutes arranging theirs in the upstairs bathroom before everyone travels together to the funeral.

When I first traveled to Poland, I took a long, long train ride and arrived in Bialystock and was taken by car to Lomza. I can remember how alien the place felt – and now that I've been there a few times – three physically and many times in my dreams – I no longer feel that it is at all foreign.

63I remember that Boshena, my Polish cousin's wife, was very proud of her family, her two sons and her four grandchildren. She told me that her seven-year-old granddaughter was a poet and had won some huge award and had been on national television.

When I went to the funeral, I met the young girl, who was about eleven or so and was very shy and quiet and didn't talk much about the poetry that she was writing. Her grandmother did though – sometimes grandmothers, even when they can be very embarrassing, are wonderful inventions. I'm glad they are around – even though neither of mine are alive any longer– I did love having them when they were here on this planet with me.

64 I went to Poland when I was a baby – I don't even really count that I was there – it was 1980, or maybe even 1979. I, obviously, don't remember it. Anyway, the area I was taken to was not Lomza, but Kieneshen (though that is not the correct spelling) where my great-grandparents were from. Apparently, I met some cousins there. In the late eighties, my sister went back with my father and met some of these cousins again. One of these cousins was at the funeral in Lomza and is a lecturer of economics at the University of Bialystock and was a nice, albeit strange (all the nice ones are strange) woman who said a few interesting and philosophical things about her visits to the woods near where she lived.

She had really wanted me to visit her there, but I had promised my German friend that we would be heading back to Germany to visit some of her college friends at Gutenberg University.

In any case, the cousin had a few pictures taken with me and said she would save them. The image of her sitting in her woods with my picture is a very "poetic one" if I do say so myself. She accused me of being a "romantic" when I gave her a copy of my anthology, and she enjoyed the title. *You too can have this beautiful life*. I enjoyed being called a "romantic" because I think I most definitely am one.

65The food that was served after the funeral service included coleslaw, as well as other traditional and yummy Polish foods. It has taken me a long time to like Polish food - I definitely did not like it when I had to go to Brockton to have Sunday dinner at my newly arrived Polish relatives apartment – the ones that my dad helped get out of Poland because the one cousin was in Solidarity and was not on good terms with the Communists. I did not like having to eat beet soup with dumplings in it – though today I love beet soup – and even go so far as to call it *borscht*.

I spoke with the extended family in broken Polish and broken English while eating the food. We were having "coleslaw conversations."

[66]*Herbata* is Polish for *tea*.

[67]During the very long car ride, I listened to some of the Polish radio stations. The American music that aired often included Leonard Cohen and Whitney Houston. The music that I found the most interesting to listen to was the Polish hip-hop. One of my favorite jazz songs is "The World is a Ghetto" and I thought about that in Poland, listening to Polish hip-hop, and even though I couldn't understand the lyrics, I enjoyed the sound. It somehow felt apt that young Poles today write rap music.

She stopped at a McDonald's for the fun of it, though, most of the time in America, Harriet can't stand McDonald's (but not as much as she doesn't like Starbucks. She really doesn't like Starbucks.). She thought it was interesting to go to the McDonald's. She, however, refused to buy anything from there although her friend did get some food and drink. Instead, Harriet bought a carton full of over-priced blueberries from a man selling them in the parking lot.

Note Bene – *a confusing narrative switch. Is this Harriet, is this narrator, or is this simply a test to make sure that you, idle reader, are not as idle of a reader as your name implies?*

[68]She wrote a poem called "Fries and a Coke Never Tasted So New" about a trip to the Turner exhibit at the Birmingham Museum of Art with the monk. The monk loved McDonald's and made her go with him for lunch to have French Fries with sweet and sour sauce. She is making a slight allusion to the other poem with the first part of this line. The second part is simply a comment on the service industry and its relatively new hold on many Eastern European countries, including but not limited to Poland.

[69]The smiles are faked with ketchup. This is a bit of enjambment that is meant as a metaphor for the pain and struggles, as ketchup is a symbol often in Harriet's poetry that refers to blood, of the New World Order, and its effects across the globe. *Zlotys* are/were the currency of Poland; even though on May 1st, 2004, Poland joined the E.U., the currency did not immediately shift to the *euro*, much to the chagrin of Harriet and her travel companion, as they had

plenty of *euros* but no *zlotys*.

[70]Before back is simple alliteration and western sunset is a double-entendre as they were driving back West into the sunset, on a late afternoon and they were traveling back to the "West," in this case Germany.

[71]This is a sort of weird one. Harriet read a bit about the engineering of the road systems in Germany and specifically about the *autobahn* and so knew about the car pile-ups that happen, although infrequently, and that sometimes involve dozens of cars.

[72]This refers to the windmill farms across Germany. Harriet thought that maybe a driver stared at them instead of the road and caused the accidents that led to the pileups; she thought if she were ever to cause an accident, which she is not planning to do, it would probably be because she was staring at the windmills.

[73]This is a line that can be read two ways: with the line above or alone. *With* simply means that the grown-ups are driving Mercedes, and *alone* simply refers to the country where Mercedes are from and where even the cabs are Mercedes.

27

Harriet was glad to have been able to go to Poland to pay her respects to her cousin, as he had been so good to her and because she knew her mother and father and brother and sisters would have gone to the funeral if they had been as close as Hamburg.

(When you think in "American terms," distances don't seem as far.)

She was sad to see her other cousin, the dead man's brother, there. She was sad because he didn't visit his brother in Poland when he was alive.

He had planned to.

He had bought a ticket to fly from America to Poland

(most likely, via London or Frankfurt)

to visit his brother. He had not seen Poland since the beginning of "The War" when he and his mother and the not-yet-dead brother were taken by the Russians to Siberia. After the war, he had come to America via Argentina.

(for you history buffs, you are well aware of Eva Peron's invite to the brave soldiers that helped defeat Nazism

    (although only temporarily. Neo-Nazis are alive and well.)

to come and immigrate to her country. Well, my cousin thought that Eva Peron was terrific. He still does. Just ask him and he will say in his very thick Polish accent how beautiful Eva Peron was. He will even blush, but you will have to look very carefully as it is very difficult to tell when he is blushing as he was burnt very badly by a flame-thrower during "The War," and his face is very pink most of the time.

But if you look in his eyes

    (unlike his brother, both of his remained intact)

you will see a smile there.

    (Yes, eyes do smile. If you don't believe me, make the person you love most in the world laugh, and then look in that person's eyes – you will see the smile. I guarantee it.))

In fact, here is a fine time to share the story of "The Brothers of Monte Cassino." But before I do, I must say two things:

1. One day, Harriet would love to work on the screenplay that tells this story. Before then, however, she needs to complete the following

screenplays:

> *The Islanders,*
> *Matilda II: All Grown Up,*
> *Geeks in Love,*
> *Adel and Peter,*
> *Fidel's Honeymoon,*
> *The Hollywood Couple,*
> *Red State Star,*
> *Taming of the Screw,*
> *Bases Loaded,*
> *The Clandestine Activities of Administrative Assistants,*
> *White Trash Intellectuals,* and
> *Life, Love, and Cooking.*

2. One of the first pieces of short "creative non-fiction" that Harriet ever shared with anyone was the following piece. She shared it either shortly before or shortly after sharing "The New Yorker's" with John Hough, Jr. and the writing club that he ran on Monday evenings in West Tisbury on Martha's Vineyard.

Brothers of Monte Cassino

Had the fire-torch singed not only his face but also his cerebral cortex, and was he now suffering under the hallucinations that he had heard other soldiers wake in the night screaming about? He would be sure to ask the British surgeon about this as soon as this battle was over, assuming that he was still alive. But still, the man thirty yards away – or thirty meters, as he was still in Italy, Monte Cassino to be precise, fighting against the fascists who hated Jews and who hated Poles and who hated him – did resemble his brother. He blinked again, more slowly this time, silently praying that this apparition of his brother whom he hadn't seen since those terrible months in Siberia would disappear. He had an important job to do, driving this tank, controlling the direction of its traversing, and he couldn't be distracted by a vision of Edward who was fighting somewhere with the Russians, probably in northern Africa. But when he opened his eyes, Edward was still there. He shook his head in disbelief before asking the gunner in the broken English that his allies had taught him, "Vat is da odder regiment that iz fighting wid us here? Ver are de from?"

His confused crewmate, worried at this non sequitur coming from the Polish driver that so rarely spoke, answered with trepidation. Fearing that this, before now, silent Eastern European was losing it, and scared that his life was in the hands of a lunatic, he said, "I dunno, why?"

Walter, now confident that his injuries were only exterior ones, yelled out, this time in his native tongue, the Slavic words falling on now-terrified ears

"Oh, ya, ya, it is my broddur," said Walter, remembering that Polish was far from being a universal language. "God in Heaven, it is my broddur."

And as the Italians were retreating, there was time for this reunion. He jumped from the tank, hitting his head on the steel above him, before remembering to open the forty pound – or eighteen kilogram, for he was still in Italy – lid that protected him from the outside world.

"Eddie, Eddie, it is me, Walter, your brother."

Edward knew the voice, though his remaining one eye could barely recognize his younger brother, now a full-grown man, emerging from this tank. They ran to one another and hugged, laughing and crying.

Drinking vodka and sharing stories, still worried about what the Communists had done to their other brother John, the two were happy to at least both be alive and together.

This reunification was to be a brief one, for there was still a war going on around them, a war that had no concern for two Polish brothers who thought the other surely dead, both here, and very much alive, laughing in Italy.

And they promised to be together again, if and when this war ever ended, they knew of a cousin in America with a farm and with work. And they hugged the strong Slavic hug, now both confident that there was something to live for.

Okay, so we should have warned you – the short creative nonfiction piece was going to be awful. *Mea culpa*. I did mention, at least, that it was one of Harriet's early pieces. Go through it and mark out the awful lines, shouting at the cliché images and criticizing the Polish accent that reads like a German one. Go ahead, I don't mind. It's good for you. I already know some of the issues that make this piece horrid, but maybe you can find some more and share them with me.

Also, in Manhattan, there is a neighborhood called Hell's Kitchen. A man born in Stoughton, Massachusetts, who works in radio, lives there and "moonlights" on Sunday brunch at a restaurant on 9th Avenue between 50th and 51st Streets. His name is John Campanario. He is related to the Brothers of Monte Cassino and learned this story recently.

28

She spent the month of August in Germany and in Poland and flew back to the U.K. when the month was over. It was then that she began to read *The Idiot*. She decided that she would read all the great Russian novels/plays

    (the ones by   Tolstoy
                            Dostoyevsky
                            Chekhov
                                and
                          Gogol)

and would take her honeymoon to Russia and take the railroad from Moscow to Saint Petersburg.

    (Harriet realizes that first she must find a boyfriend[74]

---

[74] Actually, at the time of this particular editing, Harriet has found herself a boyfriend. He is mentioned in an earlier footnote and his name still is Adel. He is still from Morocco. He is still a waiter at *Le Madeline* restaurant over in the theater district on 43rd or something near there. Though Harriet is now happily in this committed relationship, she will not be heading to Russia with her partner – anytime soon.

(and one that actually exists)

and then get into a committed relationship,

get engaged,

get married,

and have a partner that also wants to take a honeymoon to Russia and take the railroad from Moscow to Saint Petersburg.

Harriet very well might take this trip on her own one day, if the

---

Especially as she has recently learned that his student visa may have expired, making him illegally living and working in the United States and unable to leave its shores if he ever plans to come back. He is a man without a country – in several ways – choosing to remain illegally in America, which doesn't consider him a member; he is forbidden from traveling to Morocco, the country that considers him a member because he would not be able to return to the country he has been living in for the past twelve years and the country that he considers to be his home.

In fact, he is, in many ways, more "American" than Harriet is. Which is pretty funny since Harriet is "as American as they come."

Oh, yes, just a reminder. This is fiction. Of course, if Harriet was a real person, she would call the authorities and tell them that there was someone who she suspected was in this country illegally – though she would have no real proof and only have made it up because she is an aspiring fiction writer and often makes up missing details to stories of real events in order to make them more interesting in her head. The police would send her on her merry way, telling her to stop making up stories. She would be embarrassed but would make a comment in passing, "But the signs in the subways tell me to report anything suspicious..." The police officer would nod slowly and respond, "The sign does not say for you to make up stories about people because you don't have all the small details and are an aspiring fiction writer and want to make things more interesting in your head." And then Harriet would say, "Have you ever read the book *1984*?" The policeman would smile, softly, and his eyes would look a bit sad, and he would nod his head and say, "Yes, a long time ago, a very long time ago."

honeymoon gig falls through.

When she made these plans in her head, she was happy.

> (In case you haven't figured this out already, Harriet is a romantic.)

When Harriet was in England for that final week and a half, she didn't really miss the monk.[75]

She didn't even really think of him that much. She visited Birmingham, Coventry, Oxfordshire, and Devon to see some of her writer friends before having to leave for America. She met great writers that she herself writes to in a group email almost every month – nagging them about their writing and telling funny stories about her life back in America.

But when she was taking the bus from Totnes, Devon to London for her final trip to the airport, she thought about the monk. She thought about the time she had been on a bus that was going to Totnes and not leaving from Totnes, about two months previously…

---

[75] She did write him a huge letter, but she never sent it. She thought it would be better to write down all the things she wanted to tell him and that made her think of him, and to keep them for herself. Essentially, Harriet was writing a journal. She rereads the journal sometimes to remember what she was feeling and thinking in Germany, and she is glad that she never sent it to the monk.

...she had said goodbye to the monk and gotten on the bus. She felt that she was in a movie – which is a strange feeling to have when you are actually going through something.

(A lot of people that witnessed the attacks on 9/11 described feeling as if they were "in a movie"

(as a former student of psychology

(Harriet is very proud to have graduated *summa cum laude* with distinction from Boston University where she joined both Phi Beta Kappa and the Golden Key National Honors Society

(she is especially proud to have had as much fun as she did during college

(which was a lot))).

Harriet now wonders if these descriptions of personal feelings about being "in a movie" will eventually be studied.

Is there a cultural phenomenon that is prevalent today in contemporary American culture wherein individuals see reality as a reflection of film or television? If so, would this be best analyzed by psychologists, anthropologists, or sociologists?

She also wonders about Emotional Intelligence and when it will be discussed by academics and/or journalists as something that is required in American society more than in other contemporary societies[76]

In other societies, Harriet believes, it is okay to be moody or not smiling all the time, or even a bit aloof.

> (Harriet's European friends seem more able to be moody or not smiling all the time, or even a bit aloof, and it doesn't appear to affect their career or professional status.)

She sometimes thinks that America is a land of marketing – and that not being moody, smiling all the time, and not being even a bit aloof are good for marketing and for business and for the "American psyche"

(whatever that means).

She doesn't think that this is necessarily good or bad,

but she does think it is a big part of Life in Contemporary America, and wonders if it is being researched, examined, studied, or what-have-you'ed. She does not lose large amounts of sleep thinking about this question, but on

---

[76]This is touched upon in the book *Bait and Switch* by Barbara Ehrenreich.

occasion the monkey-brain does get fixated on the idea and makes Harriet wonder about it.)).)

29

She walked onto the bus

    (which

        (just like in a movie)

    was about to leave)

and didn't turn back to look at the monk.

    (she was mad at him, but we will get to that part later – after we tell what happened after – first)

The bus was completely packed

    (just like in a movie)

which was odd, because it rarely ever was.

She was crying very hard, tears were running down her face, and she couldn't stop them.

    (She didn't even try.)

She was starting to blubber--

    (that's when you cry so hard that you can't really breathe and you sort of sound like you're choking, but you're not – you're just crying really hard and your lungs ache.)

and could barely see down the aisle.

    (I am not exaggerating. This really happened like this.)

She saw a little old lady

    (Harriet adored little old British ladies)

sitting by herself and decided to sit down next to her.

Harriet smiled bravely at the little old lady

    (Harriet can be annoyingly friendly and polite.

        (She wonders how long this friendly-and-polite business will last in New York City, but isn't worried.)

And some people could possibly consider it fake, but Harriet thinks there's no need to be rude to people, especially to strangers

(Sometimes, she is rude to family or friends

(and, especially, to her little sister Maria who lives on 52nd Street in Manhattan, between First and Second Avenues.)

but thinks that they know her, so it is different.).)

before sitting down. Harriet continued to cry, loudly. She was so sad that she wasn't even embarrassed. She just cried and cried and let herself keep crying.

It was at this time that she was very glad to be on a bus in England and not on a bus in the United States. Harriet is very confident predicting that in the United States someone would have asked her what was wrong and made her explain why she was crying. Harriet didn't want to talk to anyone

(which must have meant something, because Harriet usually LOVES to talk,

(especially to strangers),)

and so was very glad to be in England. After a few minutes of crying, she tried to sleep, but the pain in her stomach was very strong. Harriet

Elizabeth Dembrowsky

hadn't felt that pain for many, many years.

(you know the one, right? The Ache[77]?)

---

[77]Harriet wrote a poem called "Ache" and dedicated it to her friend Gloria. Her friend Gloria went through a very difficult period when Harriet was in England; the difficult period involved ending a long and long-distance relationship that went on over three thousand miles over three years. Anyway, Harriet wrote the poem "Ache" describing in vivid (or at least Harriet would like to think that it is vivid) detail what the pain in your stomach feels like on those nights when you can't sleep because your heart is thinking of someone whose heart is not thinking about you.

I don't recommend this, however, really, to be completely honest, Harriet always wanted to feel this, because she always wanted to know for sure that her heart was capable of being broken. Harriet is a little strange.

Anyway, I would have loved to include this poem however, it is missing. I think that it may be on a disc somewhere in Harriet's parent's house, but those discs are all PC's, and now that Harriet is a Mac girl, as is her roommate and her little sister, and as she no longer has a job where she can put her disc into the computer and open files, even if the discs were with her in NYC and were not in her parents' house somewhere in the mess of boxes of letters and books that her parents let her store in her old bedroom, the bedroom that her oldest nephew refers to as "his bedroom," she would still not be able to open the files.

Anyway, the poem talks about your desire to rip open your own stomach to remove the cyst of hurt. It talks about you floating above you, looking down on you and on the pained and squirming body below that is you, about where the pain is physically located and all that "David Copperfield kind of crap."

Anyway that poem is MIA. The one on the next page is not.

My Monk

Dreams happen when your eyes are closed.

Dreams only happen when your eyes are closed.
It is the moment after waking when you smile
        to feel his hand resting on the curve of your hip.

The smile is on the inside. It spreads
from the part of your body you would call a soul
if you were that-sort-of-girl,

butters the insides of you in one smooth, easy swipe;
ten toes arch, inhale gallons of air,
your lungs now the size of zeppelins.

Then, woosh----------
wakedness sets off a spark, ignites, and leaves you –
a pile of ashes lying in now-twisted sheets.

His soft, steady hand melts away;
the scent of his body on your sheets only the alligator brain
        playing its crooked, crocodile tricks,

leaving you wishing you had set your alarm ten
        minutes earlier: forcing you to jump directly
from flying to Saturn into the shower

skipping fully
the moments of
sleeping with a ghost.

I guess I should make it clear. I NEVER had a physical relationship with the monk, even though Naomi, my publisher, wanted me to. Oops, I mean "Harriet" never had a physical relationship with the monk. Remember – I am simply a narrator of this novel, and narrators of novels, at least this one, are not capable of having a physical relationship; this narrator doesn't even have a physical self.

Anyway, just so that you don't get any wrong ideas, I thought it beneficial to include the disclaimer – who knows, maybe monks sue for libel if they want to, and Harriet definitely doesn't want to be sued for libel, especially by a certain monk.

Elizabeth Dembrowsky

Harriet thinks that each and every poem should not necessarily be autobiographical, that some should attempt to really reach a reader, to describe something so that a reader, a stranger to the writer, can read it and can go "Yes! Exactly, that's it! That's exactly it! I'm not as alone as I've always thought I was! What a relief!" And others can simply describe an event, artwork, moment, or idea that the reader can read about and then think, "Hmmmm, well, I've never thought about it this way. How interesting. I'm not sure if I agree, or even fully understand, but there are two neurons in my brain that just made a connection where previously there was none. These two neurons might end up a part of a long and complicated series of connections, but perhaps no impulse will ever again travel over this particular synapse. Oh well, it's always nice to make more connections in one's brain. Or, hmmm, maybe it's not, maybe it's better to have fewer connections, but solid ones.

Oh, I think I need to take a nap, but first, I'm going to reread this little, strange poem here…"

30

Harriet wanted to curl into a ball

    (or the fetal position)

and just cry and cry and cry and cry away the pain in her stomach.

She tried to sleep for a long time and even managed to do so for a bit, but then a strange thing would happen. She would wake up and start crying again

– it was awful.

She tried to eat her sandwiches

    (the ones that British Harriet had made for her)

but even cried into her sandwich.[78]

---

[78] She wrote a poem about that, too.

Finally, a few hours into the journey, Harriet was resting and no longer crying and instead trying to read a book. The little old lady in the seat next to her opened her big black bag and took out some chocolate. She opened the chocolate bar and broke off a chunk of chocolate. She turned to Harriet and offered her the chunk of chocolate and said, "Would you like some chocolate?"

Harriet nodded and said, "Thanks." She took the chocolate and smiled at the old woman who turned away and looked out the window.

* * * * * *

For the next several days, on and off, Harriet would be overcome by the pain in her stomach. It happened most often when Harriet was in bed, about to fall asleep.

National Express

Tears fall shamelessly to a lap of mozzarella
Soggy as the tea towel hanging on a faucet.

Hollywood wants her money back
And places an embargo on your kind.

Mother love never hurt like this
Aborted love, an unfine romance.

Strong and broken –
Down on the side of the M5
With no petro in the tank
And no directions back.

But sometimes, this pain would come to her in the middle of the day when she was doing her writing, making a salad, or on a walk.

Harriet called her friends in America more that week than she had in the entire rest of the year that she was in England. She tried to tell them what she was feeling and tried to learn why. No one could tell her.

Some people laughed

> (but not in a malicious way, instead, in a sort of "Oh, Harriet, you are so dramatic" way)

and told her that, in time, it would go away.

Her friend Gloria and her friend Brenda were very "good" at these times. They never laughed or said that, in time, it would go away.

They listened.

The monk was still in England for a final few days, but Harriet didn't call him

> (not even once).

She had given him a letter that she thought explained her feelings and didn't have anything more to say.

Harriet

(as mentioned previously)

is a romantic. She often gets herself into trouble because she creates scenarios in her own head that contain no semblance to reality. People in her life often criticize her for this; however, she enjoys it. Harriet honestly feels that her life is better with these created scenarios, because if Harriet were to look honestly at her own life – sometimes it would be very grey, dreary, and depressing – like the skies of England.

Instead, she thinks about possibilities, all sorts of possibilities.

One of these possibilities was that the monk would read the letter, realize he was making the biggest mistake of his life, and instead of getting on a plane to Russia, he would get on a bus to Totnes and would come to where Harriet was living, knock on the door, and when she opened it, he would tell her that he loved her with all of his heart and soul.

(Harriet watched too many romantic comedy movies when she was a young adult

(In fact, during her "Hardcore Feminist Stage"– she used to say that she was going to sue Hollywood for all the false promises they create

(though Harriet was very aware that just as *Crime and*

> *Punishment* would not be responsible for forcing Harriet to commit murder if she had, that Hollywood was not responsible for Harriet buying into the whole idea of "romantic love" and "fairy-tale endings.")).)

This did not happen.

But that did not stop Harriet from having silly hopes.

Leo wrote her that a friend of his was coming to America and that he wanted Harriet to go to New York and to meet her there.

> (Harriet was not yet living in New York)

Harriet already knew a bit about her and agreed to meet her, but not in New York. She wrote him that the friend was welcome to come and visit her in Massachusetts and she would be her tour guide for Boston, Cambridge, and the White Mountains of New Hampshire and that Harriet could find her a place to stay with one of her friends in New York, but that she herself had neither the time nor the money to go there.

The friend wrote that she would come. The friend wrote an email in Romanian-English, and Harriet smiled reading it, thinking of how the monk first wrote when they were in England.

In fact, the emails reminded her so much of the Romanian-English that the monk first wrote, that Harriet secretly thought that it was the monk that was coming to America and not his friend. Even when she was waiting for the bus to pull into South Station in Boston, Harriet secretly thought the monk would be there.

Instead, a very shy and quiet Romanian girl-woman emerged from the bus. And they were immediate friends.

Harriet never admitted out-loud her secret hope that it was the monk and not a very shy and quiet Romanian girl-woman that was to get off the bus that day

> (though maybe one night when she drank too many beers, she might have told one of her close friends)

and for the most part even kept it from herself

> (Like a lot of people, Harriet keeps secrets from herself
>
>> (Therapists call this "denial"
>>
>>> (but it is more involved than that
>>>
>>>> (These secrets people keep from themselves sometimes become lies and sometimes there are lies that people tell themselves.).).).).

However, he has since written her emails almost every other month, each time he leaves the monastery, (which is located in Moldavia

(a province of Romania))

and travels to Bucharest

(which is the capital of Romania)

(where the monk used to live and where his mother and father and little sister still live).

He tells her silly things most of the time, but also writes about his mother, who is sick with cancer and asks Harriet to pray for her.

Harriet does actually pray for the monk's mother even though she doesn't really believe

(She does, however, believe that prayer is capable of having positive effects if the person who is being prayed for learns about the prayer.

Her favorite professor from Boston

(actually, she had two. The other favorite professor

(named Jean Berko-Gleason)

did great work in linguistics

  (interestingly, some of her great work was done in Romania

    (but with gypsies and not with economist/poet/monks))

and had a fantastic, caustic wit

  (and would say things like "I'm from Iowa, or Ohio, or one of those places.")

and was very down-to-earth for such an accomplished and bright woman.)

used to talk with Harriet about the positive effects of prayer. Even though both Harriet and her professor were atheists

  (Harriet was an atheist Catholic and her professor was an atheist Jew),

they were familiar with the studies about prayer and positive thinking and the correlations with better physical health.

  (In fact, Harriet's Aunt Andrea

    (who used to be called Aunt Andy until she wanted to be called Aunt Andrea)
was recently very sick with cancer, but believes strongly

in the benefits of positive thinking

(even though she too is an atheist)

and is doing much better than the doctors had expected and thinks that part of the reason why is indeed because of all the people that were wishing her well

(including the monk).))

Harriet went so far as to ask her best friend

(Brenda)'s

mother to pray for the monk's mother.

She also asked her little sister

(who is a "practicing Catholic"),

and even went to church with her parents in order to pray for the monk's mother.

31

The monk sent Harriet an email that bothered and confused her, questioning her plans to move to New York City, hinting that she would find it unsatisfactory and warned her that she needed to "visit her heart"

(Harriet has made many moves in her life – so many that some might say that one of Harriet's hobbies was "moving," – but the move to New York,

(or at least Harriet thinks so)

was the biggest of her life, because she really wants to "make it there." Maybe only to "make it" so she can retire to a small town, like the one she was raised in, but she wants to "make it" nevertheless.)

and was very nervous about that

(especially when Harriet was never negative to the monk about any of his plans (even though she honestly thought he was running away from life by joining the monastery)).

She was also bothered and confused that he lectured her to "visit her heart." Her problem

(she thought)

was that she did indeed "visit her heart" and that it had not worked out very well for her.

(she also thought that maybe when the monk wrote for her to "visit her heart" he was referring to G-d.

(The monk had once told her that he thought she should become a nun

(In fact, he later told her that the first time he had seen her, that was what he had thought

(which is very funny, because the first time that Harriet saw the monk, she thought he was cute).).

but when Harriet wrote back,

"as for me – visiting my heart – not really sure what you mean. if it has something to do with you thinking i am supposed to become a nun, then i must be clear. i might never be a mother, but i remain open to the idea."

the monk then accused Harriet of bringing up the "nun" issue claiming that he was never referring to that.

However, Harriet is pretty confident that she would not make that up.

> (seeing as how never in her life had anyone told her that they thought she should become a nun.

> **The above statement is a lie**. In grade school, Harriet was extremely moralistic and used to lecture her classmates constantly. They accused her of being "holy" which isn't quite the same, but she doesn't remember every single detail or every little thing that has happened during her twenty-seven

>> (yes, 27 – a bit too old for these shenanigans)

> years on this planet, and figures that one of them must have told her to become a nun.

> Harriet is pretty confident that she remembers him saying that.

> (in fact, Harriet remembers being in Birmingham walking in the rain from the Ikon Museum

>> (of Contemporary Art)
>> to the Birmingham Library when he said it to her.)

Harriet does remember thinking about that very often and getting so frustrated.

Harriet did bring it up on a different occasion.

She and the monk had met in London for a few days.

This is one of the very weird things about her friendship with the monk. It was as if they were dating, but without any physical contact.

> (though, on occasion, she would kiss him on the cheek
>> (like at the beginning of their Easter Break when she was going to Spain and he was going back to Romania for a few weeks
>>
>> or when he arrived in London and she was there waiting for him at the airport or when she was going on a bus to Birmingham from London and he took

> her to the bus station)

> or pinch him

>> (Harriet is a pacifist, yes, but an aspiring one, and sometimes the monk would get her so aggravated that she would pinch him on the arm.

>>> (yes, Harriet is very aware that this was extremely immature

>>> (but who really wants to be mature all the time, anyway?

>>> (not Harriet))))).

They would eat lunch together, and he would carry her soup bowl to the table, and she would get napkins and pepper and spoons for them both. They would buy each other awful coffee from the coffee machine on the ground floor of the Humanities Building.

They would watch movies together and spend lots of their time talking to one another on the Fourth Floor of the Humanities Building in the computer room that the two of them named "Home."

> (in fact, they would refer to meeting the other one at "Home" when they were with other friends or colleagues and giggle together about it.)

They would argue about politics and literature and Madonna's career moves.

They would talk about friends from home.

    (The monk had two very close friends

        (Andrew and Adriana),

    whereas Harriet had many

        (and the monk was critical of the number of friends she had)

            (he was often jealous of the attention she gave to other people

                (like when she would talk to the boy who cleaned up the dishes after she was finished eating her soup with the monk

                    (it made Harriet very mad, because he was not her boyfriend. It made her think of Robert Browning's poem "My Last Duchess"

                        (Harriet has wanted to write a poem in response to Browning's on behalf of the last duchess.).)

or when she would talk about her best friend

(Brenda)

(but, nowadays, Harriet thinks that the monk was just being over-dramatic when he would be jealous of Brenda))

and of Harriet having her attention split in so many different directions.)))

and most of hers were very close as well.

(but that is because Harriet has spent a lot of her time keeping up friendships with people

(which can be very difficult at times)

that she has met along the way.)

The monk's two close friends are a particularly interesting case. Andrew has also joined the monastery, and Adriana is now a close friend of Harriet's.

(Yes, you are right! Adriana is the shy and quiet Romanian girl-woman who visited Harriet and took a bus from New York to Boston.)

(Adriana and Andrew are both very smart writers and critics from Romania.)))

She wrote the monk an email about how much she had been upset about his lecture and asked him to "let her go."

She wasn't really sure what that meant, but hoped that he could give her "his blessings" and let her get on with her own life.)

32

All she ever really wanted from the monk was for him to say something like, "Harriet, you are a nice and smart young woman. I am glad that I met you. You made me realize that America is more than Britney Spears and George Dubya. Thank you. I wish you the best."

<u>Another lie!</u> That was not all she ever really wanted from the monk.

She also wanted:
- flowers
- candies
- for him to remember her birthday
- for him to tell her that he loved her-
>that he loved her more than anyone on the planet, and,
>
>that he wanted to spend the rest of his life trying to make her happy.

Instead, the last thing he said to her was:
>"When we pray, we are never far apart."

Harriet wanted, at that moment in time, to say really mean things about his G-d, but decided not to. Instead, she started to cry and got on the bus.

It is probably wrong to expect and want things from people, but Harriet

> (like most people)

does it anyway. Really – in the deepest corners of her heart, she knew that she and the monk would never really have worked out.

This part is not a lie. Harriet really did know these things in the deepest corners of her heart. She just kept them hidden there maybe because:

- her landlord was a jerk,
- she didn't have very much money,
- the Great American Novel was not as easy for her to type out as she had expected,
- it rained a lot in England,
- the dollar was not doing very well against the pound,
- George Dubya and the Neo-Cons seemed intent on destroying the world, and
- a few other things.

> (though she did think about moving to a small village in Romania and being the wife of an Orthodox priest and teaching the little children in the village how to read or having the monk get his priesthood degree

(or whatever it is called)

(Orthodox priests are supposed to get married.)

and move to America and work on his Ph.D. on "The role of Christian Orthodoxy in Contemporary Art Movements of the 20th Century" and editing Harriet's novels.)

She knew that not only were they from two very different cultures, but that they were both too much the same and too different, in ways that would not be complementary.

She did actually know this.

However, *knowing* and *feeling* are two very different things.

It would be easy if there was a **Good Guy**

    (or **Good Girl**)

and a **Bad Guy**

    (or **Bad Girl**)

in this

    (and every)

story.

However, things are not that simple.

Harriet could go through a list of acquaintances and friends and put them into either:

| **Harriet is Right** | **The Monk is Right** | **Neither is Right** |

columns. But that wouldn't prove anything. Life is not a vote.

And its events are not easily classified into neat columns.

And, really, it doesn't matter if there is a **Good Guy**

    (or a **Good Girl**)

or a **Bad Guy**

    (or **Bad Girl**)

> ***All that is left is the rest of your life.***

Harriet tried on more than one occasion to cut the monk out of her life

    (or at least to lessen the role he played in her life)

    (or the time that they two spent together)

(or simply the time Harriet spent thinking about the monk).

but was not very successful.

The most recent time that she tried to do this, the monk wrote her an email that was titled "you must be." The first line of the email read "12 years old at most."

Harriet was very upset at this. She had

    (thought that she had)

opened up to him and explained in clear and concise language that the monk still had a strong effect on her and that she didn't like the effect. She wrote about her heart and what was inside of it, and that she needed him to "let her go."

What she had wanted was for the monk to give her "his blessing" and let her live her life. She wanted him to write something like "Good luck, kid, you're going to need it out there."

    This was not the first time she had done this...

She and he were eating soup together, discussing poetry and Madonna's recent career moves. In fact, on this particular late afternoon/early evening, Harriet was helping the monk write a letter to potential publishers of an anthology of writings from young Romanian writers.

    (the monk was considered by some literature critics in Romania to be the leader of a new generation of poets. These poets were called "The utilitarian poets", and the monk had won a scholarship to attend the university in England and serve as editor and translator for a collection of these writings[79].

---

[79]This anthology of poetry was actually published by Heaventree Press, based in Coventry in the U.K. and is called *no longer poetry*. Harriet did a bit of work for Heaventree Press in the U.K., co-teaching workshops to students, refugees, and asylum seekers, and a collection of the writings that were generated in the workshop were published in an anthology called *I Have Crossed an Ocean*. Harriet even has a short, and, she thinks, very bad, poem published in there. She wanted them to publish the following poem instead:

"...and the wisdom to know the difference."

It is dangerous to read newspapers.
Each time I hit a key
On my electric typewriter,
Speaking of peaceful trees

Another village explodes.

—Margaret Atwood, 1968

It has been two weeks
since I have read an American paper
It has been two long weeks
of intentionally realizing that I am addicted
to something I have no control over.

I glance quickly at a table that isn't mine
and see an outline
of a headline

Instinctively, I read –
C.I.A. Director Resigns.
I smile

then cringe
noticing that a foreign newspaper
doesn't even have the decency to
write "American C.I.A..."

Somehow, Harriet helped with this project by going over the English translations and making different suggestions for words and phrases

(This reminds Harriet of her favorite translators — the married couple living in France — he is an American and she is a Russian and together they translate Dostoyevsky and win awards)

(except that this couple is married and one did not decide to join a monastery).)

and letting the monk know when specific words had different meanings from what he had expected.)

She was relatively good at writing these sorts of letters and had earned herself a fair amount of grants and things of that nature

(for art projects, and photography projects, and film, and even for writing projects).

They took a break and spoke instead about why the monk wrote poetry.

He told her that each poem means things on different levels

(as do most poems)

and that one of the levels was always religious.

Harriet thought about this and wondered if he was trying to convert people through his writings.

She asked him about his opinion on free will and whether or not, if he was given the power, he would choose to make everyone in the world believe in what he believed in.

This was a very, very important question for Harriet because, at this moment in time, she was very scared that all along she had been helping a propagandist who wished to force his beliefs on others.

She asked him, "Please, tell me – you don't believe in Rapture, do you?" He asked her what Rapture was. She explained that it is the idea that Jesus will come to the earth and take all the believers to heaven and leave all the unbelievers to live in a hell-on-earth. She told him that many Born Again Christians in America

(and around the world)

pray everyday for Rapture to come.

(there are books written about it – awful fiction about the world with the heathens left behind.

(actually, Harriet has never read any of these books and is not being fair when she criticizes books she has not read

(sort of like the ex-President and ex-Chancellor of the first university where she studied

(Boston University),

(John Silber)

   who

      (according to the book *You Can't Be Neutral On a Moving Train* by Howard Zinn

        (a gorgeous old man who still

          (even in his eighties

            (or that is how old Harriet thinks he is, she is not positive and wishes not to be sued for libel)

        continues to fight for the things he believes in

            (like civil rights and a fair system for workers and a cleaner environment)

        with a smile and with a laugh.

        He is a very inspiring man

> > (or that, at least, is Harriet's opinion
>
> > > (but she is not alone in that opinion)).))

once was sued by a professor from the English department on the grounds of sexual discrimination

> (or something like that
>
> > (Harriet doesn't want to get sued on the grounds of libel).
>
> Harriet isn't really sure how the story goes.)

for not giving a particular professor tenure. This professor was an expert on Jane Austen. The president of the university accused Jane Austen of being the "matriarch of mediocrity"

> (or so the story goes)

And,

    (although Harriet loves Jane Austen

        (and while in England kept expecting to meet her own Mr Darcy),

    she does think that that insult that the president of the university used is a great one).

There ended up being a court case regarding the woman's application for tenure. During the court proceedings, it turned out that the president of the university had never read any of Jane Austen's books.

Harriet found this very funny.

    (especially as she and the president of the university had disagreed on very many policy issues

        (The president of the university is credited with having made the statement:

        The more democratic a university is, the worse it is.)

> (It was rumored that the political science department faculty had an on-going battle of a discussion regarding what third world dictatorship most paralleled the leadership style of the president of the university
>
>> (Cuba, Iraq, and Libya were at the top of the list, at the time).)

and even went so far as to make their differing opinions known to one another.

> (In fact, Harriet saved the response letter from him, and she was so pleased that he was so "honest" in his reply that she hung it on her wall for a period of time)

As Harriet had been your typical bleeding-heart liberal type all through college, she was very different from the president of the university who was a very conservative and practically-minded gentleman. She was so disturbed by one of his practices that she wrote him a letter explaining why she was opposed to his decision and also that he should be aware that many alum shared her opinion and would very likely refuse to donate money to the school.

Harriet knew that the president of the university was a very practical man

> (in fact, it was partly due to his practicality that the scholarship that Harriet studied under was made possible)

(Harriet knew this, but also knew that she would not be deserving of the scholarship if she did not engage herself in the university and its practices and activities, even if most of these were philosophically the complete opposite of those of her scholarship providers

> (the president of the university and two other people were involved in the initial creation of her scholarship
>> (the other two people were

Cardinal Bernard Law and Masschusetts Ex-Senate Leader William Bulger

(making the trio a very controversial group — which is a whole different story and not one that will be explored at this time)

(or anywhere in this book)

(sorry, but maybe another time)))).

This is what Harriet considers true scholarship to be and is discouraged by what she feels is a lack of critical thinking and analysis on the part of many in her peer group. She fears that her entire generation will collectively be without a strong skill set of critical thinking abilities and thinks this will be a very sad thing.

She fears a future that lacks critical thinking.

She also fears the following:

- cats eating her after she dies alone in her apartment in New York City

    (although Harriet has none of the following:

    - her own apartment in New York City
    - cats
    - a plan to ever get cats),

- Falling through the grated sidewalks in The City,

- the effects of celebrity culture on the development of a thoughtful and insightful personality,

- war,

- turning into Condoleezza Rice.

She does not fear the following:

- the I.R.S.

  (as any and all mistakes she has made in preparing her taxes have been accidental)

- death,
- heights,
- spiders,
- snakes,
- scorpions,
- lions,
- tigers,
- bears,
- witches
- ghosts,
- "bad neighborhoods,"

- rich people,
- enclosed spaces,
- socialism

And she knew that he tended to run the university as a business. She wrote that she for one would not be contributing funds to the university.

Now, here comes the funny part.

He wrote her back a letter discussing his reasons for his decision.

Okay, so that part is not funny, but wait — it is coming.

He made a three-point argument clearly explaining his position.

However, Harriet was still disappointed, as she found his logic flawed.

33

However, she was pleased that he did respond to her.

(She liked to have people respond to her, irregardless

(And, by the way, I agree with those who continue to fight for the word *"irregardless"* to be officially welcomed into American-English.)

of their opinions.

(One of her favorite quotes is Voltaire's, or, at least he is credited with:

I don't believe in a word you say, but I will fight to the death for your right to say it.))

And she was especially pleased with what the university president added as a postscript.

This is the funny part; thanks for being so patient.

As for your threat of economic boycott. I am not impressed. In my experience, individuals who threaten not to give have never given in the first place.

    (or something like that

        (Harriet no longer can locate the letter.).)

The great thing about his postscript was that he was right.

She had never given. In fact, she hadn't planned to give.

Now, don't be mistaken. The above does not mean that the president of the university "won" because Harriet still strongly believes that the logic was flawed in his counterargument.

However, he is a practically minded conservative gentleman, and she is

    (or at least was)

a bleeding-heart liberal.

Still, she has respect for him. Even if they are convictions that she does not share, she does appreciate that he is

    (or at least appears to be)

consistent.

(People often find this a strange trait of hers.

(She often admires people that she disagrees with strongly.

(Harriet admires the following people:

- Bill Gates

- Martha Stewart

- Madonna

- George Soros

- Ralph Nader

- her best friend, Brenda

She does not admire the following people:

- George W. Bush

- Rupert Murdoch

- Britney Spears

- her temporary boss at the brokerage firm she briefly worked at in Manhattan

- people who kiss their dogs on the face.)

Sometimes Harriet likes strange things about particular people

(like the following:

- that Pope John Paul II refused to give Madonna's daughter a special baptism

- that George W. remembered that Poland had sent troops to fight in his

   (ILLEGAL AND IMMORAL)

   war, and mentioned it during a debate when John Kerry forgot to do so

- that Queen Elizabeth II leaves the country when she is supposed to sign a bill that she is philosophically opposed to

- that her aunt's husband

   (who is no longer married to her aunt)

   once called her aunt in Massachusetts from L.A. and sang into the telephone:

> *I just called to say, "I love you."*
> *I just called to say how much I care...*
> and that it made her aunt laugh.

> (Harriet doesn't always know if these stories are completely true, but she likes to think about them and wonder about why she likes certain things about certain people))

which may have been part of the reason why she liked the movie *Amelie* so much. The movie had tons of little details about people.

Harriet used to ignore the details and only focus on the concepts and the ideas and the "Big Picture" but she learned to love the details.

She learned to even celebrate them.

She loves details like –

- the sound that she makes when she walks in high heels

- the feeling of hot tea when it has just been poured into a mug, and she leans over it, and the steam fills her nose

- smooth writing pens

- when people snort as they laugh and then try to ignore that they did it.

She loves a lot more details but this is not a book version of the movie *Amelie*, and we need to get back to the story at hand.

(or at least get closer to getting back there...)

The monk loved details. He was a poet. Usually, poets are "all about" the details.

Harriet liked when the monk would drink coffee and when he would lift it to his mouth, and it would steam his glasses.

Harriet thought it was the cutest thing about the monk.

The monk hated it.)))

The monk heard Harriet define Rapture, and he said, "Of course that is what I want. For Jesus to return."

Harriet was shocked.
    perturbed.
    upset,
    distressed,

agitated,

bothered,

dismayed,

disturbed,

grieved,

hurt,

put out,

troubled,

worried.[80]

She couldn't believe that she had spent all this time with this person who couldn't wait for the day when he would be taken to heaven and she would be stuck in hell-on-earth.[81]

---

[80] Kudos to Harper Collins for publishing such a nice, helpful, and "cute" *Pocket Thesaurus*

[81] Okay, now that Harriet is really serious about becoming a writer and an artist and a photographer of graffiti, abandoned buildings, and her friends caught in fabulously alive moments, she has let herself become more free to think and, sometimes, say some pretty odd things. For example, the following story:

The day the Pope died was a rainy one in New York City. Harriet had gone out the night before and had acted irresponsibly and foolishly. The next day, hungover and missing her keys to her apartment on a weekend that her roommate was out of town, Harriet woke up and got out of the bed in the hotel she had stayed in a few blocks from her own cozy and locked apartment with an awful hangover and a need to get herself to the Brooklyn Art Museum to meet Gloria (the biologist or geneticist or what-have-you-ist) and her boyfriend (the Williamsburg-living, pool-playing, California-raised, part-time artist assistant, part-time artist, fulltime boyfriend) to see the Basquiat exhibit, which, by the way, was splendid. After the trio split up, or the couple split up from Harriet, Harriet wandered around the neighborhood during a light rain. She walked to a liquor store to buy a pack of cigarettes, though she soon found out that they didn't sell cigarettes in this particular liquor store where a television was on and reported that the Pope had died. Harriet felt very strange. It was one of those

Elizabeth Dembrowsky

moments that her dad had referred to when he told her "once a Catholic, always a Catholic." She walked around in the rain, thinking about the people of Brooklyn and of the dead pope. The rain increased. The wind increased. Harriet had no umbrella and decided to alter her initial plan of waiting until seven in the evening before going to a friend's apartment to meet her and see her apartment and get ready for a night of dancing, and instead decided to visit her little sister in Manhattan and stay in a warm, dry place.

She walked to the subway, used her Metro Card, and began what was to become a strange trip back. The subway car she was on had an extra-crazy crazy lady who spoke loudly, initially to the amusement and later to the annoyance of the other travelers. She spoke about the MTA police and how they harass homeless people and especially her. Initially, Harriet listened to her, thinking that she was right, that the MTA police probably in fact did harass homeless people, but as the extra-crazy crazy lady went on, Harriet realized that the woman was mentally ill. She talked about all sorts of strange things about her suitcases and about the fires that were started in the subways by the MTA police and were blamed on the homeless women. She told the passengers that the MTA police would set mattresses on fire and that they would blame these incidents of burning mattresses on the homeless women.

The passengers were, for the most part, tired and wet and not in the mood to hear this woman's very loud rantings, but the subway stopped in between two actual subway stops and remained there for a dreadfully-long ten minutes during which time the extra-crazy crazy lady continued to talk nonstop. At one point the car moved ahead and then stopped a few yards later. Five minutes later, the train moved again. Stopped again. Moved again. This hellishness continued for a full thirty-five minutes before stopping at a particular stop, still in Brooklyn. The doors opened and the car remained in the station. A conductor came over the loudspeaker and said that because of a fire at Wall Street, the train was delayed. The extra-crazy crazy lady began yelling about fires and the MTA police setting them and blaming it on homeless women; now every passenger felt particularly hellish. Finally, the woman sniffed loudly and said, "Can you smell that? They have set another fire, another fire, I can smell it now." The fellow passengers were extra tired and collectively felt powerless sitting in this car. A minute or two later, the passengers began to sniff, for they too could now smell what indeed smelled like a fire.

At this point, Harriet got very frightened. She started thinking about the Pope's death and about the extra-crazy crazy lady who had predicted the fire. The smell of fire terrified Harriet, but no one else on the train looked remotely concerned, except for the extra-crazy crazy lady who continued ranting about fires and mattresses and the MTA police.

Now, as Harriet wants to be a writer and artist and such, as mentioned previously in this particular footnote, she does on occasion nowadays allow her mind to wander, letting her brain focus on silly, unlikely and very strange scenarios--like the following.

The Apocalypse has come and gone. Rapture occurred at the moment of the Pope's death, and here she was stuck in hell-on-earth with the other non-believers.

For a full twenty seconds Harriet thought about this. What would life be like in this place? New York City subways as a hell on earth. Fires and stopped subway cars and extra-crazy crazy ladies – for the rest of eternity.

On occasion Harriet prays. This was not one of those times. Instead, she simply thought about how she was going to manage living on a post-Apocalyptic planet. Two minutes later, the conductor asked the subway passengers to disembark because the car was no longer going to be going to Manhattan. Harriet smelled the fire more strongly as she got onto the platform and began to walk up the steps. As she and the other passengers filed up the stairs, several firemen in full gear appeared, walking down the stairs toward the platform. Harriet again thought about the Apocalypse – about dying here in this subway station in a fire, but she did not panic. Instead she thought, "Well, that's too bad, I thought I had a good fifty more years on this planet. This little game ended too soon. I thought I might even bring a kid or two or twelve into existence and one day retire to a house by the sea and take up knitting and belly-dancing at age seventy-five. Ahh, this is too, too bad. I still haven't even seen Machu Picchu. What a bummer!"

Harriet didn't panic and think about needing to live and not wanting to die. This is a strange thing about Harriet: she isn't afraid to die. She is afraid, rather, to be on this planet and forget to live. She thinks that is worse than dying. Harriet created a fictional character named Katherine that reminds Harriet of herself in many ways, or at least reminds Harriet of who she used to be in a lot of ways, who thinks or at least is thought to have thought that she was afraid to "spend even one minute on this planet not fully living."

In any case, here comes the funny part, Harriet walked to the top of the stairs and looked up and saw the world's most beautiful fireman. She made direct eye contact with him, and he smiled at her, coyly, and she almost fainted. She decided very quickly that life in a post-Apocalypse world wasn't going to be so bad after all.

One hour and one half later she was on 52nd Street in Manhattan between 1st and 2nd Avenue, ringing the buzzer of her little sister.

She got up and ran outside.

Harriet may have been overreacting. Maybe he spent time with her because he thought she was open to his ideas and beliefs and whatnot; however, Harriet was so hurt and angry and couldn't believe that a man-boy as smart and sometimes-nice as he was could hold such an awful belief. She couldn't understand it.

(But before she did, she excused herself.

(Even when she gets very upset, Harriet can usually still be polite.))

She ran outside and started to cry. She went to the store across the street and bought a pack of *Marlboro Lights*. She immediately smoked one as soon as she got outside. She sat on the steps, and she cried and cried.

How could this be? she thought. *How could someone really believe this?* Someone she cared about. Of course, she knew it was a diverse place with many different beliefs; that was something she adored about the world –

Different ways of trying to make sense of something that didn't make sense. She found it wonderful – usually.

She had read a lot about Buddhist and Taoist beliefs when she was in high school (as did a lot of high school kids in America

> (or at least the kinds of high school kids in America that enjoyed learning about different ways of thinking).)

And when she had first given up on Catholicism, she had looked to the Episcopal Church, before turning that aside as well.

Her father had even pushed her towards Judaism – wanting his daughter to choose a faith that had standards, a strong code of ethics, and the Ten Commandments.

She had an aunt and uncle who had "found Jesus" in Alaska and were even Born-Again Christians.

But hearing the monk confirm her fears nearly broke her heart.

She returned to the table and sat down, finished the editing and excused herself. She walked home that afternoon, crying for almost the whole four-mile walk.

Under normal circumstances, she enjoyed the walk. The scenery, the countryside, all of it made her pinch herself with joy over actually being in England and living this wonderful storybook of a year.

Usually, all of it made her pinch herself with joy; however, not this time.[82]

Elizabeth Dembrowsky

[82]Harriet did, however, write a sort of strange poem about the walk.

yellow brick road

it's all your fault
you planted it there
it grew and grew
then was impossible to cross
but i did
(the impossible is easy for me.)

his big toe kept me grounded.
his big toe always does that —

though the rest is a big big mess —
scattered things that mean to others
not to me. nothing to me —
just his big toe, that means something to me.
it means a lot.
it means something to her too and to him but
most to me.
drunk dancing bears laughed at me at mile 3.

One day, she was telling Leo about how much she loved riding the bus, what with it being a double-decker and all, but also adding that she hated to wait for it; she started walking, possibly after Leo suggested it, home most nights, and it was such a lovely time for her to be with herself and her thoughts and to reflect on her day. Leo would say that she was praying at these times, but Harriet continues to call it reflecting. She would listen to her iPod and hear Frank Sinatra or Folk Implosion and be happy, sort of homesick, but sort of happy. Leo had challenged her to walk home very, very late one night – like at one or two a.m., and he had even offered to walk her home; in retrospect, this was very, very strange. Anyway, she did it alone, and it was freezing, and she ended up writing a silly, almost nonsensical poem about it, one of her first pieces that was even moderately influenced by Leo's style – with images that perhaps make sense to no one but the author and the random reader who might intuit his or her way into the mix.

My Monk

i was too cold to fight –

they just laughed and i proselytized to them –

they pretended not to understand.
(bears do that.)

they were too warm –
i borrowed their coats –
gave them my cigarettes. – i quit – i told them.
they laughed again –
i lectured again,
this time
about work ethics –

they interrupted and called me a protestant.
i said: no – i'm just always right.

they laughed at my talking about freedom –
one of them punched me,
right in the gut.
i told him: that wasn't very nice

i will have to make some phone calls.

he laughed and said:
well, it isn't very nice of you to preach the way you do.

realizing their coats were on my back, i ran away.
they puffed after me but i was already home.

and because it was tomorrow i tried to be quiet
about the talks i had with myself after that – which
was difficult. (they are usually the loudest of all.)

i woke up screaming about the rain
and how i had gotten the point already.

it's all your fault.

34

By the time she arrived home, she was mentally exhausted. She ran over and over again in her head their conversations about faith. She called her two closest friends

(Gloria and Brenda)

and neither of them was home, so she tried to sound brave while leaving messages on their machine, but, in the end, cried as she spoke.

(Later, she got an email from Gloria wherein Gloria told her that hearing Harriet cry made Gloria cry. She wrote that she was the one that was supposed to cry, not Harriet

(which taken out of the context of their friendship must sound strange, but what she probably meant is that she was the one that usually was upset, and it was Harriet that would be the eternally cheerful one).)

That night she wrote the monk an email.

leo–

i dont know how to say or write this, but i think i have to stop spending so much time with you. even when i'm not with you, i have to stop spending so much time with you, actually.

i hate that i have a heart b.c. it always betrays me. i wish i could be happy just thinking, but i cant. what i'm trying--and failing--to say/write is that i had totally fallen madly, hopelessly, deeply in love with you – b.c. i am stupid and before you even said that you were going to become a priest i knew it.

maybe it's b.c. i'm scared, maybe it is b.c. my expectations are too high – but whatever the reason, i search the world and seek out the worst people ever to fall for and then i do it. and i did.

but before i drive myself absolutely insane, i have to stop. i have to live in reality and not in my head – though the world in my head is a much better one –

so, i know it is coming off really oddly, but for myself – once in my life i will do this – i have to stop doing bad things to myself/my heart and i have to stop torturing myself.

i will still help you with this anthology – i think it is a wonderful 'experiment' and i love being a part of bringing something new to a wider world – it's what i try to do with my life-and i love helping you with it.

however, i can't let myself be around you so much – it is very very bad for me. and this isn't about Jesus and hell and redemption – it's about me. me not making people into my 'surrogate boyfriend.' me not fictionalizing things. me doing what i need to do to not hurt me. this probably seems overly dramatic, but i'm a woman, it is what we do ;)

anyway, i'm not going to be a big freak about it, ignore you or anything, i just need to tell you that i can't do this to myself. i hope you don't get mad at me or think that i am a bad person/friend. if you do, i'm sorry.

i am working on sunday until 6 or 7, not sure, and i can come to the p.c. room after that to help you do some further edits on your anthology.

–harriet

Harriet thought it best to be honest. Leo wrote her back, needing to talk, and she wrote him back that she did not want to talk.

She wanted to stop whatever it was that was wrong with her heart and her head, fix it, and move on.

And she did.

    (For a little while.)

But things eventually went back to the same way that they were before; the two of them spent time together and laughed and learned and wrote.

Soon enough, her heart was breaking again. She had fallen deep into a trap of enjoying her time with him.

It would be funny if it wasn't a true story.

It would be such a funny romantic comedy –

**The Silly Little American Girl
and a Romanian Economist/ Poet/ Monk.**

But it is a true story, and there is no happy ending and no Hollywood set.

    (Harriet finally truly understood the lure of the movies. Things are better there)

(or, if they aren't better, sometimes they are so much worse than real life that they can be comforting.)

Harriet wrote her friend Gloria and asked her advice. Gloria is a very levelheaded person

(sometimes)

(though Gloria does have some strange

(and very endearing)

idiosyncrasies

(like

- hating cats
- thinking everything is a conspiracy
- always thinking she has cancer
- believing in aliens)

and often can come off to other people as being aloof and even curt)

and tends to see things as they are and not as how she wants them to be.

(Sometimes, for people

(like Harriet)

who can have a difficult time seeing things as they are, it is very nice to have a close friend who is very good at seeing things as they are.

(This is often called "having perspective" but you probably already know that.)

Sometimes, these types of friends form symbiotic relationships with individuals

(like Harriet)

who have a hard time with living in the real world. These practical types of people actually enjoy befriending dreamers.

Maybe it is some sort of charity work.

Or, maybe, they simply derive pleasure from knowing that there still are people in this world that are still dreamers.)

Gloria wrote Harriet back and told her to "be careful" of her heart and that she was free to enjoy spending her time with the monk, but she had to remember that he was going to become a monk, and that monks do not get married to idealistic, wide-eyed American girls

(not even in the movies).

Harriet was happy to get that advice, remembering the adage:

Advice is what we ask for when we know the answer, but wish we didn't.

Knowing what to do and doing it are still two very different things.

And

(yes, you guessed it)

Harriet was not careful of her heart.

In her defense, however, she did try. And, even for a while, she thought that she was being careful of her heart and simply enjoying spending time with someone as smart and witty

(and sometimes – mean)

as her monk.

Her monk

A strange phrase.
A strange phrase, indeed.

However, he was to everyone that knew her – "her monk." Her friends in America laughed, kidding, "Harriet, you must seek out these people. How do you manage to find them? I mean, it is as if you intentionally seek out these unavailable men and fall for them."

Elizabeth Dembrowsky

Harriet didn't have an answer.

Some things don't have answers.

Or at least they don't have answers that are easy to find and speak or write about clearly and concisely.

Maybe that is why poetry exists – because as much as some poets would like to claim it, poetry is not written in clear and concise language.

After it was all over, and Harriet had come back to America.

Harriet had went back to America.

Harriet had returned to America.

Harriet had come back to America, she looked back and wondered, "How had it happened?" She wondered what had led her to England to not only not find her rich, British aristocrat or her fellow American who had left America for a while, but she found a man that was preparing to dedicate his life to a G-d that she didn't believe existed.

She shouldn't have been able to be jealous of a person, or being, or Creator that she didn't believe existed, but somehow she was.

Would it have been easier for her if the monk had told her that his heart belonged to a girl in Romania?
YES! It would have much easier. She could have asked questions about

this girl in Romania and found out about the types of things that he did for her to make her smile. She would find out her name and her hair color and what her opinions were on Madonna's recent career moves. There would have been answers to these questions, and these answers could have been provided in clear and concise language.

But there was no girl in Romania. There was not even a boy in Romania

>   (though Harriet did raise her eyebrows over the constant talk and adoration of the monk's best friend who was going to join the monastery with him).

There was simply a G-d that Harriet didn't believe in.

I must offer an apology. Today is June 10, 2005. It is 1:58 in the afternoon on Tuesday. It is hot and I am writing from a desk that has a red coffee mug filled with strong coffee with hot, frothed milk on it. There is also a printer-scanner-copier that was purchased several years ago from the QVC. Embarrassing, ehh? Who admits these things? Anyone in a work of fiction can admit anything. Fiction is a fantastic disclaimer. More people should pick it up. There is a picture of the/a shy and quiet girl-woman from Romania standing in front of a gorgeous and decrepit cottage in Chocorua, New Hampshire. The house has a red door and is brightly painted. There is also a stack of books that includes but is not limited to *The Graduate* by Charles Webb, *Puppet Plays, Divan Poems, Prose Poems* by Federico Garcia Lorca (and published by Sheep Meadow Press, in Riverdale-on-Hudson (which is actually Riverdale, which is actually the Bronx), New York), *The Collected Shorter Plays of Samuel*

Beckett (the Grove edition), *Touring Lower Manhattan: Three Walks in New York's Historic Downtown*, *Madonna: An Intimate Biography*, and *The Chicago Manual of Style*. There is also a reddish tube of lipstick and a red, cloth address book.

> (Red. If I was a filmmaker, either a European or Steven Spielberg during the making/editing/use of limited color of the girl with the dress in *Schindler's List*, I would find the use of the color red to be interesting. I would intend it to have some hidden sort of meaning. However, in this case, it is merely a coincidence – that is, if you believe in such things.)

Out the window a scene includes half of a tree, rows of windows, several air conditioners, lots of bricks, a bit of a blue but slightly cloudy sky, and the effects of a slight breeze on the leaves that are on half of a tree.

An invitation to a *Ceilidh* is taped to the wall behind the printer-scanner-copier as are several printed photographs of graffiti. One of the images includes part of a sidewalk and a wall that reads, "my pony is over the ocean." Another says "Scabies" and was taken in Totnes, Devon. Another reads "Empires Fall." There is also a letter from Yolanda Miller of the September Agency whose first lines read, "I was pleasantly surprised and pleased with your treatment and first half of your screenplay: MATILDA– ALL GROWN UP. I would be happy to review the rest of the script."

There is a note written on April 9th that begins,

Hello
to my favorite
Cosmopolitan Girl.

There is a poem entitled "Riding a Bicycle to Istanbul" whose last two stanzas read:

you'll find that contrary
to reports in
norton's anthology,
jack kerouac is alive.

if he says he's from bonn
and an anarchist
studying spanish,
don't believe him – i didn't.

There is a quote from someone named Andy Murphy that reads, "i am in Buenos Aires and the city had charm seeping from its cracks."

What, pray tell – hmmm, is that really how that phrase is written – or is it simply one word – I might get myself a copyeditor one of these days– does a physical description, and a dry and boring one at that, have to do with an apology?

Nothing.
It was an attempt at procrastination.

Mea culpa. Mea culpa. Mea maxima culpa.

In my attempt to be a post-post modern writer/narrator/thingamajing, I lost the plot.

Mea culpa. Mea culpa. Mea maxima culpa.

I forgot the map. I forgot to give pertinent, or at least helpful, or at the very least chronologically-sound, information.

The monk.

When Harriet first met him, he had no plans to become a monk.

Ha ha ha. You big jerks! Laughing at the idea of Harriet sending a man running to the monastery to get away from her. Ha ha ha. Very funny. There is a word in either German or Yiddish that I cannot think of right now that means taking joy in others sadness or misfortune. If you are one of those types, you probably are laughing.

But Harriet did not send him to the monastery, he was on his way there already, but Harriet did not know this.

Or did not admit this to herself.
Or did not admit this out loud to anyone else.

She knew he was religious. It was one of the first things she learned about him, along with the following facts:

- He was cute and tall and too skinny.

- He hated her writing, or at least said to her on the first workshop of the year.

- He had published two volumes of poetry previously in Romania.

- He was high-strung and very spoiled.

It was not until January of 2004 that Harriet learned for sure what his plans were for the future. The way she found out was very simple. She was there when he was asked, "What are your plans for the future?" He answered, "To become a priest." Later, he added the monk part.

"To become a priest." Harriet was shocked. But she was out at a restaurant at the time, one that served fantastic food, not an easy thing to find in the Western Midlands of the United Kingdom, – and it was her mother, not one to beat around the bush (visiting Harriet for the week) who asked the question.

Immediately feelings came to Harriet's stomach as if her organs had dropped through the floor, not unlike being on a rollercoaster .
Her mother looked at her and Harriet quickly blinked three times – a bit of extra water in her eyes that she hadn't noticed before. She did not look at her mother at this moment; instead her eyes darted quickly in her mother's direction and quickly away from her mother's direction as if her eyes wanted to signal to her mother – her eyes wished to say something like:

Wow! Figures, eh? Comedy or tragedy, dear Mom. Which is this? Did you know the Indigo Girls sing: you've got to laugh at yourself or you spend your days crying. *Hey, dear Mom, let's laugh. That's right – you and me, Harriet's eyes, let's laugh. Because, really – it is pretty funny. That G-d-guy, He got her good, this time, didn't He?*

She simply listened to his answer.

35

Inside – her heart burst. It wasn't until this very moment that she was sure that she had a heart. Of course, she had a blood-pumping, circulatory heart. And, of course, she had been sad before – she had seen a fair bit of death, dying, suffering, poverty, injustice, and cruelty for a middle-class white American girl raised in New England – more than a fair bit, in fact.

However – you might not know this, oh intelligent and insightful, yet open-minded reader – but there are two love hearts: One for the sadness of humanity. The other is specially built to be broken at a nice restaurant in January in the Western Midlands of the United Kingdom by a Romanian poet when he says he plans "To become a priest."

Somewhere, the story is told differently, tongue in cheek, mocking our dear, sweet, wide-eyed Harriet. But not here. Here it is tragic and sad and we can understand why Harriet lost her bet to quit smoking with Brenda. We can completely understand why, after she drove the Romanian-poet-now-planning-to-become- a-priest back to his dorm and she drove her rented-for-the-week little-four-cylinder car back to 57

Beehive Hill in Kenilworth, Warwickshire, she stopped at the convenience store and bought herself a ten-pack of Marlboro Lights. We can understand why she turned up the music on the radio, lit a cigarette, and cried as she drove the five kilometers from the university campus to 57 Beehive Hill. We are full of empathy for our little twenty-first century Job. We might even get a little sad on her behalf.

A few people in Harriet's life told her

- that she should tell him about how she felt –

- that she should tell him not to join the monastery –

- that she should tell him that they could make a life together and together serve his G-d through their love for one another

(some of Harriet's friends can be a bit romantic in their thinking themselves).

Harriet thought about that.

She never read *The Thorn Birds*, and she hadn't

(at least at that time)

seen
(or read)

Oscar and Lucinda

(though she did later see the movie.)

(and later went to a literary event in NYC

(her first on arrival[83])

---

[83]Her second event was to hear the author of *The Fuck Up* and *Suicide Casanova* read and to get a copy signed for her roommate. He was very nice to Harriet, that Arthur Nersesian fella, and let her tell him what she wanted him to write on the inscription – though he added an f-word or two, but Harriet didn't mind, as it was part of his shtick to use profanity/obscenities so loosely. He wrote a little cryptic message about Danielle staying away from the beet horseradish.

The night before, or maybe two nights before, Danielle and Harriet made a grand dinner including pieroigis, sausages, sauerkraut, cabbage, and yes, beet horseradish. It was a stupid thing, but Danielle, accidentally, she claims, took the beet horseradish off Harriet's plate rather than from the still nearly-full jar. Stupid and silly, but ehh, life ought to be those things every once in a while.

Her third was to go to an event hosted by *L Magazine* wherein five short-story writers read 1000 word (or less) shorts at a bar in the West Village.

Her fourth was to see Kinky Friedman read and talk about his campaign to run for governor of Texas. Harriet hopes that he wins.

In the book, *Kill Two Birds and Get Stoned* by Kinky Friedman, the character Clyde Potts tell the character Walter Snow, "Writing a book is like falling in love or getting to sleep or finding a taxi in the rain. It'll come to you, but first you have to let it."

Harriet has since gone to another author event. She went to hear Ian McEwan read from his new novel *Saturday*. Harriet was thrilled to hear him read in the flesh; he was just as she had envisioned him, geeky and bookish-looking and with the type of British accent that Harriet had expected – though she doesn't know the name for that particular accent; however, she is very confident that it is most definitely not a BRUM accent; she thinks it could be the Oxbridgian accent, but isn't willing to bet money on it, and not simply because she doesn't have enough of it.

She was interested in seeing Ian read for several reasons:

1. She had written an essay describing one of her own short stories and had used one of his novels, *Enduring Love*, as a major model for showing the passage of time and had wanted to see if he would speak about the passage of time in fiction and the in-text cues that a writer gives to the reader. (He didn't, and Harriet was too shy to ask and had also assumed that the majority of the fans there wouldn't be interested in such a seemingly obscure question.)

2. She had read many of his novels and had read a section of his newest one in an issue of *The New Yorker* and, for the first time in her life, felt as if she was "on top of things" in relation to the literary world and such. For that reason she wanted to be there. (She was actually interviewed by a Master's in Journalism student from N.Y.U. and was very happy to see the woman write down so much of what she said, though Harriet doubted that it would ever go to print. Harriet was still pleased to have her ego stroked in that way. Remember, ego and Ego, there is a difference.)

3. The monk! Yes, annoyingly enough, he haunts Harriet even in a city as un-monk-like as New York. He had first introduced her to the works of Ian M and, in fact, had given her a copy of *Enduring Love* as a gift and had inscribed it-

To Harriet,

Two ways of missing the point,
for a soul that I pray gets it right,

Leo

Exeter 2004.

Or something like that. Harriet lent the book out, to Gloria, biomolecular chemist, researcher or whatever, and Gloria hasn't given it back yet.

where Paul Auster

(a neat novelist—who somehow Harriet still can't fully get into) (who is friends with Don DeLillo

(and is married to a writer

(whose name Harriet cannot remember[84])))

gave a very interesting lecture about the role of inanimate objects in film at Hunter College

(where Harriet's little sister is currently working on a degree in Art History)

that was hosted by the Creative Writing Department that happens

---

[84]But whose letter Harriet filed at her old job working for Mr. Stanley Moss of Stanley Moss and Co., Sheep Meadow Press, and New Yorker contributor fame. Again, have no worries, Mr. Stanley Moss let Harriet go, as in "did not decide to hire her" and give her full health benefits – she is still far removed from the literary establishment, although she is right now on Martha's Vineyard writing this, and will have A VERY DIFFICULT TIME GETTING THIS BOOK PUBLISHED. This isn't a ploy, dear reader (notice that the narrator has softened enough to not refer to you as "idle," he/she/it must be trying to soften you up for something, like a raise in his/her/its allowance, or a confession of having forgotten to pay the phone bill, or making up for having forgotten your wedding anniversary, or worse--your name), to make you feel sorry for Harriet. Don't. Harriet doesn't feel sorry for herself. Harriet is happy to be her own woman, even if she is in a bit of debt and doesn't have the money to do the sorts of things she would like or to contribute the amounts of money she would like to the organizations that she would like. She has to believe that she will be successful, even if her level of success is definitely on her own, constantly altering, terms. To quote Billy Joel, "Either way, you wake up with yourself."

to be run by one Mr. Peter Carey — author of *Oscar and Lucinda* (and several other award-winning books)).

And she wasn't at all into the idea of having an affair with a man who was "married to G-d." Harriet found even the idea very tacky. She has no real issues

and pauses in order to ask her Catholic and wonderful parents to skip the following few lines

with the idea of having sex without being married.

(In fact, she has never been married and has had sex--

(but she isn't going to go into details about with whom and under what conditions.)

But she does have huge problems with the idea of infidelity. And a promise to a G-d that she doesn't believe in is somehow just as sacred of a promise as one to a spouse.

For that reason -- married men and monks are most definitely off her list of potential sexual partners. COMPLETELY off the list! Women are too, no matter what her friends may say.

And she also decided that she wasn't going to "fight G-d" for her monk. She was pretty sure she would lose.

And, furthermore, she was afraid.

What if she won?

Would there be a special hell built for a woman who tempted a man who had planned to promise himself to G-d? It seemed so much like the biblical Eve or Mary of Magdalene.

(two women

(by the way)

who Harriet always felt got a very raw deal in the whole patriarchal system of organized religion which was part of the reason that she gave up on Catholicism

(the other parts included

- she wasn't so sure about transubstantiation and couldn't really find any evidence of it in the Bible. She always thought that the man called Jesus was speaking figuratively when he said that stuff about taking his body and blood and eating and drinking it.

(though the idea of a G-d asking us to eat his body and drink his blood so that we can have him in ourselves is actually a very beautiful idea – once you get over the initial feeling of "eww, gross, cannibalism.")

- the fact that the Pope was so sure that he was infallible. She found that lacking in anti-hubris[85].

- she didn't particularly like the weird sexual issues that somehow float around Catholics. Sex is great. It is a celebration of life – it isn't something to be ashamed of

  (or at least that is how Harriet thought about it)

- she didn't really believe in G-d.

Now, it is worth our seriously getting off the track. The idea is, however, still related to the monk, in that it relates to G-d.

(And, as much as Harriet didn't tend to think of the monk as a man of G-d, because he made her so upset so often, the monk would like to think of himself as a man of G-d and, in fact, has essentially decided to spend the rest of his life, trying to be, or being, a man of G-d.)

However, the idea itself, although relating to G-d, does not relate to the monk or writing or poetry or England.

It relates to a young woman named Harriet

---

[85]Yes, we are still all aware that anti-hubris is not a word.

(yes, the same Harriet)

who lost her faith when she was a teenager.

It isn't that strange a story.

You might know it yourself; in fact, you might have experienced it yourself.

All that faith-in-transition jazz, wherein a person raised within a particular faith reaches adolescence and begins to question the role of religion in one's own life, the validity of religion, the purpose.

Usually, the adolescent survives fine and enters into the faith-by-conviction stage that – at least for many – is supposed to last until death.

Unfortunately, in the case of Harriet, this stage never occurred.

She remained transitioning
and transitioning
and transitioning.

She asked her religion teacher about it.

She asked the priest that had baptized her.

She asked friends.

She even asked her parents.

She would find out about other people who were rumored to have lost their faith as well and ask them questions.

She once even called a boy who thought that the football players at his school had put her up to it

(they hadn't)

she called and asked him "Do you believe in G-d?"

He didn't, but his reasons were stupid, and so Harriet moved on.

Her parents worried and gave her books on Judaism, hoping in their open-minded way that she would at least find answers in a different traditional and long-proven religion – even if it was not any form of Christianity.

But Harriet was not converted. If there was no Jesus, then there was no G-d and there was no point to any religion....
except as a tool to control the masses.

(an opiate, even. And, yes, Harriet did fall victim to a brief stint as a Marxist, but please forgive her, she followed a cute boy there, and soon left.)

She thought about slavery in the South in early American history and about how helpful it was for slave owners to introduce Jesus to the slaves – a man that promised a better next life for the poor and the good, providing a metaphorical glass of warm milk before bedtime to an oppressed and abused people.

How helpful to use religion to keep a population in line.

Harriet converted to agnosticism.

She still went to church every week, if only to prove that it wasn't because she was lazy that she had stopped believing in G-d and sat in the pew silently when everyone else went up for Communion.[86]

Harriet's mom thinks that the old ladies that enjoy gossiping thought that Harriet was on drugs or something. This was also the time of Harriet's life in which she found it necessary to dye her hair colors like blue, purple, and green

---

[86] Now if you are Catholic, skip this part, because you already know this stuff--or should. The Liturgy of the Mass includes a recreating of the Last Supper of Jesus. There is a part of the service where the priest, playing the part of Jesus, takes the bread and the wine and changes it into the body and blood of God. This is a big deal. It separates most Protestant religions from the Orthodox Christians and from Catholics. Most Protestant sects, and there are a lot, don't. It is a very big difference. Wars are fought over it. Or have been. These days wars are still being fought on account of different people's beliefs of what religion is supposed to be. In fact, there is a poem that Harriet wrote called "The Christian Right is Neither" but I'm not going to include it here. It isn't a very good poem. The idea is nice, what with a cynical look at those that kill in the name of Christ and a call for pacifism around the world and what-not, but lyrically the poem needs a lot of work and really there isn't too much alliteration, imagery, metaphors, or anything of that ilk in the piece.

(though the green was quite an accident).

(The town that Harriet was raised in

> (that her father and his two brothers and his three sisters were raised in
>
> and their mother and their mother's two sisters and their mother's brother
>
> (but not their mother's mother, because her mother was born in rural, eastern Poland
>
> (or the Ukraine))

is a rather provincial one.)[87]

But really, neither Harriet nor her mother cared what people thought. In fact, they both found it sort of amusing that people can continue to be so dumb that long into their time on this silly little planet of ours.

---

[87] I do not wish to offend the residents of Stoughton (a.k.a. Toughtown, U.S.A.), Massachusetts with the use of the word provincial.

In fact, not only do I not want to offend them, but I want to impress them. I want them to read this book, either take it out from the library or buy it. Furthermore, I want them to buy a t-shirt, or baby tee, or spaghetti strap tee, or a raglan from White Trash Intellectuals that says Toughtown, U.S.A. across the front. These shirts have not been printed yet, but this book has not been completed yet either, so we shall see which happens first. We shall see.

My Monk

However, G-d never visited Harriet while she sat in the pew waiting for the parishioners to receive Communion. She moved towards atheism. She felt guilty about this. She went to a priest for Confession and when it was time for her to tell her sins, she said,

"Well, I...I...well, I don't believe in G-d."

Furthermore, I wish the residents of Stoughton, Wisconsin, to do the same. I would use the word bucolic, but too many housing developments have been built there in the past ten years and the bucolic character of the town is now gone.

Charming is not appropriate either as physically the place is actually rather banal, though there are some nice wooded areas and ponds and a few old, colonial houses with charm, but overall the town is not charming.

Funky is definitely not right either. There is a main street that runs through the town that seems to grow a few new chain restaurants or other establishments each year. In the town center, three major roads come together--forming a hellish traffic center for those not familiar with the area. Funky is too hip for this place.

Overall, Stoughton (a.k.a. Toughtown, U.S.A.) Massachusetts is a good place. Hell, it made Harriet (and her roommate, too). And all Harriet's dad's brothers and sisters and his mom and Harriet's brother and sisters and Harriet's best friend Brenda and Brenda's husband and two of Harriet's nephews and Harriet's friend Mara and some other pretty rad people.

And so, if you are told that the only two good things in Stoughton, Massachusetts, are a strip club named Alex's and a pizza joint called Town Spa, understand that the person who tells you this is incorrect.

The priest told her to say five "Our Father's" and ten "Hail Mary's" as a penance.

Harriet stopped going to Confession.

Harriet now has grown up enough to know that few people actually do really, truly believe in G-d, but they just decide that life without a G-d is a pretty miserable place and that they may as well believe.

Harriet still doesn't think that these people are right, but she does spend fewer nights staring at the ceiling and wondering about this.))

And Harriet may be a lot of things,

    (like   scatter-brained
                  full of energy
                  way too honest for her own good
                  inventive
                  friendly
                  a friend
                  an aunt
                  a daughter, sister, cousin, niece
                  writer
                  student
                  adult-in-denial
                  train-rider

bicycle-rider
smoker
drinker
walker
swimmer
small mountain climber
standard stick-shift driver
traveler
beginning gardener
dog-liker, but not lover
pool-player
graffiti photo-taker
trouble-maker

The quick brown fox jumped over the lazy dogs.

(just checking to see if you were paying attention)

(once, while in undergraduate school, Harriet

   (who readily admits to being a nerd)

submitted a paper on the "Audio Skills of Third-Trimester Fetuses"

   (which was actually very interesting

      (well, to Harriet at least))

with this line in it to a teaching fellow that Harriet was convinced was not going to read the paper in an attempt to prove her hypothesis. The paper came back to her with an A grade and with no comment or marking regarding "The quick brown fox jumped over the lazy dogs.")

but a temptress has never been one of those things. And though Harriet tends to reinvent herself every few months

(with such superficial things as a new hair color and style or more serious things like a new career path or a completely different way of looking at the world)

she found no reason for herself to become a temptress. She was probably more scared that she would fail.

(Remember, Harriet is very, very human – she is full of foibles and weaknesses and fears – like of failure or rejection

(though she has gotten better at failing and is no longer as afraid of rejection

(when one decides to become a writer one ought to lose a fear of rejection as it can be very, very detrimental to one's career. In fact, it is essentially a death wish to one's career unless one is born with literary contacts.))

and still somehow believed in romantic ideas that don't involve failure or rejection, but instead involve soul mates and connections-without-words and a completely fictionalized view of life and love and combining the two.)

One may wonder:

> ***Why didn't Harriet didn't take better care of her heart?***
> ***Why did she let things get this bad?***

Harriet blames G-d for this. She blames a G-d that she doesn't believe exists for making her fall in love with the monk in order to teach her a lesson. Harriet was never really sure what that lesson was, but she was determined to try and learn whatever it was.

Harriet didn't learn very much other than the pain that comes when love is not returned. If Harriet ever doubted her own humanity – this pain made her completely cognizant of it.

It was not something to study in a book, read about, write about, analyze – it was something felt in a harsh and very real way.

Maybe G-d did test her. Proving His existence to her, or at least trying to – with Harriet it can be very hard to prove things for sure. G-d knows this. He knows this for sure. His little 21st century Job-ette is quite the little difficult thing when it comes to proving His existence to, but G-d loves a challenge. He also loves Public Television and is sore at the Republicans in America who are cutting funding for it. He also enjoys sailboats and seagulls, though he sometimes regrets having given seagulls the ability to shit while flying. He also enjoys the prayers from children – He listens to every single one. Sometimes, He even saves them and replays them when He needs to smile. Sometimes, though, when He needs to smile, He simply pushes away those clouds and stares down at one Ms. Harriet Zabrosky. He has never not smiled when He looked down at her. Sometimes He smiles and shakes his head, thinking, "Oh, no, not again!" or "What is she doing this time?" and sometimes He smiles and laughs so hard that He snorts and pretends that He hasn't. Sometimes He even cries, but He cries with a smile in His eyes. Remember, you too can smile in your eyes.

Maybe one day Harriet will meet the monk again. Maybe they will become friends and laugh at the follies of a young hearted American woman with wide-open eyes, and her monk.

Maybe....

Acknowledgements

I must first and foremost acknowledge Naomi Rosenblatt, Creative Director of Heliotrope Books. Her patience, intelligence, faith, humor, and talent are so inspiringly strong that even I don't have words for it. Her commitment to this project breaks every record I know of.

Thanks to Patricia McNamara for making this *shidduch*. And thanks to Michael Fancello, President of Heliotrope, for believing in it and to Claire E. Keys for her incredible drawings in type.

This would not have been written without the encouragment of my mother, every step of the way throughout my entire life.

My proofers/critics – Dumitru David, Danielle Powers, Sally Jane Kerschen-Sheppard (did I spell it right?), Anne Eichinger, Mara Sullivan, Keshia Corban, Dolores McKeough, Harriet Josefowicz, Fran Sommers, Sarah Cavallero, Lily Lodge, Tony Brescia, Ellen Rowett and Bryan Fitzgerald – have saved many a future reader from unnecessary irritation.

To my legal counsel Peter Catalanotti, Paul Kleidman, the Volunteer Lawyers for the Arts, and my father –

To my Romanian monk and all our common friends, particularly Hats, Ro, Alex, David, Stefania, and Adriana –

To all the real and fictional people that have helped me along the way. You know who you are....*Toda raba*.

About the Author

Elizabeth Dembrowsky has written and directed several plays, including *love is the proof*, *The (Irish) Wake*, *Thirteen Degrees of Insomnia*. She was born and raised in Stoughton, Massachusetts and now lives in New York City with her fiancé. This is her first novel.

www.ingramcontent.com/pod-product-compliance
Lightning Source LLC
Chambersburg PA
CBHW071650090426
42738CB00009B/1477